MAMA, GET THE HAMMER! There's a Fly on Papa's Head!

BARBARA JOHNSON

Word Publishing
Dallas • London • Vancouver • Melbourne

MAMA, GET THE HAMMER! THERE'S A FLY ON PAPA'S HEAD!

Scripture quotations used in this book are from the following sources:

The King James Version of the Bible (KJV).

The Holy Bible, New International Version (NIV). Copyright © 1973, 1978, 1984 International Bible Society. Used by permission of Zondervan Bible Publishers.

The New American Standard (NASB) © 1960, 1962, 1963, 1968, 1971, 1972, 1973, 1975, 1977 by The Lockman Foundation. Used by permission.

The New King James Version (NKJV). Copyright © 1979, 1980, 1982, 1990, Thomas Nelson, Inc., Publisher.

The Living Bible (TLB), copyright 1971 by Tyndale House Publishers, Wheaton, Ill. Used by permission.

The personal letters shared in this volume are based on actual mail received by Spatula Ministries. All mail received by Spatula Ministries is considered available for inclusion in ministry-related materials and products by Barbara Johnson. Names and identifying facts are changed to protect the identities of the letter writers and their families.

Library of Congress Cataloging-in-Publication Data

Johnson, Barbara, 1927–
    Mama, get the hammer : there's a fly on papa's head / Barbara Johnson.
        p. cm.
    ISBN 0-8499-3417-6
    I. Title.
PN6162.J54   1994
814'.54—dc20   94-21895
                                        CIP

Printed in the United States of America

7 8 9 QBP 9

To all the darling, caring folks who have encouraged me and been the ones to lift me up, I humbly dedicate this book. May it act like a boomerang for them: Having blessed me with their letters and their love, I hope they will find their love has boomeranged back to them in these pages.

As we refresh others we ourselves
will be refreshed. (See Prov. 11:25)

Contents

Acknowledgments

Many of the quips, quotes, jokes, stories, and poems used in this book have been sent to me by supporters of Spatula Ministries, a nonprofit organization designed to peel devastated parents off the ceiling with a spatula of love and start them on the road to recovery.

Sometimes these items arrived in the form of clippings from magazines, newspapers, church newsletters, and books, or simply as funny stories shared between friends. I appreciate all of them; they have brightened my trips to the mailbox and added joy to my days.

I've tried very hard to track down the original sources whenever possible, but in many cases it just couldn't be done. I apologize if somehow I have included an item without giving proper credit; it certainly was not intentional. I will be glad to make the necessary attributions in future printings whenever I learn of changes that are needed.

The letters used in this book are based on actual correspondence I've had with hurting parents, but most letters have been edited and facts have been changed to protect the identities of the writers and their families. In a few cases I have requested and received permission to use real names and facts, and I thank those persons for sharing their stories so graciously.

I extend special thanks to the following individuals for allowing me to use their materials:

The zany title of this book, *Mama, Get the Hammer! There's a Fly on Papa's Head!* is from a song by Frank Davis and Walter Bishop. Copyright © 1961 by Southern Music Publishing Company, Inc. Copyright renewed. All rights reserved. Used by permission. International copyright secured.

My friend Ashleigh Brilliant, of Brilliant Enterprises, has graciously allowed me to use several of his witty Pot-shots throughout this book. Each is credited individually, but I want to thank him here, too, for being so willing to share his humor to help those who hurt. More information on Ashleigh Brilliant Pot-shots may be obtained from Brilliant Enterprises, 117 W. Valerio, Santa Barbara, California 93101.

Ruth Harms Calkin for allowing me to use her poetry on pages 66 and 172.

Gretchen Jackson Clasby for allowing me to use her darling "Sonshine Promises" drawings on pages 88, 120, 157, and 171.

Ruth L. Clemmons for permission to include her essay "When You Lose a Child," in chapter 4.

Dr. Peter Gott for allowing me to adapt elements from his column, syndicated by Newspaper Enterprise Association, for "Medical Confusion to Tickle the Funny Bone" in chapter 1.

Pat Hanson for sharing the quips and love notes from her delightful calendar, "Pat Prints."

Robert Hastings for his permission to reprint "The Six Realities" from *The Station and Other Gems of Joy* in chapter 7.

Evelyn Heinz for sharing her poem titled "The Alphabet Prayer," reprinted in chapter 6.

Liz Curtis Higgs for permission to use her favorite casserole recipe (see page 21), reprinted from *Does Dinner in a Bucket Count?* (Thomas Nelson, 1992) as well as her slogan used as the title of chapter 1.

Dick Innes for his poem, "Never Waste Your Pain!" reprinted in chapter 5.

Anna Jean McDaniel for her poem, "Whatever, Lord," reprinted in chapter 4.

The Helen Steiner Rice foundation for her poem, "The Gift of Friendship" in chapter 5.

Sandy Ritz, R.N., for letting me adapt her cartoon, "Ode to Burnout" for the Introduction.

Suzy Spafford, creator of Suzy's Zoo, for sharing her spirit-lifting illustrations on pages 131, 135, 152, and 173.

Larry Thomas for permission to use slogans from his *Remarkable Things* catalog throughout this book.

Sherrie Weaver for her Updated Witticisms scattered throughout the Bugaboo Busters.

Norma Wiltse for her poem "The Garment of Praise," reprinted in chapter 8.

To all of these thoughtful folks, I say again: *Thank you!*

Introduction

Mama, Get the What?

*R*eaders of mine know I use some off-the-wall titles. But this time you may be thinking, *Barbara has been playing with her rain stick too much! She must be ready for "LA-LA LAND."* On the other hand, if you're the philosophical type, you might be looking for some deep, spiritual meaning behind *Mama, Get the Hammer! There's a Fly on Papa's Head!*

Actually, I chose this title because it's zany and comical, adapted from a country-western song I found somewhere.[1] My goal is that folks will pick up this book and say, "Here comes Barbara again . . . this one looks like pure fun!"

So I have to admit there's no "deep" meaning in the title of this book, except for one thing: Humor is a powerful force, and anything that makes us laugh in the face of life's adversity is valuable. A good motto is:

> LOVE MAKES THE WORLD GO 'ROUND,
> BUT LAUGHTER KEEPS YOU FROM GETTING DIZZY.

So, that's what we hope this book will do for you—provide plenty of smiles, chuckles, and laughs. Of course, there is a purpose in all this zaniness—to encourage you wherever you are

1

as you experience life's ongoing trials. Every day my mail reaffirms the fact that life is hard, and while some folks wish they could just "erase themselves," they have to keep going.

A woman wrote to tell me that a year after her wedding, an injury put her in a wheelchair, shattering her career as an aerobics teacher (she used to be a track star). Her crippling injury also dissolved her hopes of having children—how could she care for them if she was unable to walk? And she wondered, "Do you have any advice for me?"

A mom with three sons wrote that one son had been in the homosexual lifestyle for fourteen years, and about a year ago another son decided he also is homosexual—this after being married and having a beautiful daughter. He is a Christian and knows what God's Word teaches, and the mother asked, "How can this happen?"

Still another mother wrote that she lost a daughter who was killed in an accident while she was away at college. Meanwhile, her son now "leans toward homosexual companions," and his twin brother lives too far away to see her very often. She suffers from diabetes, and to top it off, her husband left her for a younger woman.

The letters just keep coming. One lady said she felt as if she had been living in a set of PARENTHESES since learning about her son's homosexuality. "I keep trying to move the parentheses," she wrote, "and they keep stretching out, and I am still in these horrible parentheses in my life!"[2]

If a set of parentheses doesn't quite describe where you're at right now, maybe you relate better to a PIT or a TUNNEL. You may just be going into your tunnel; maybe you're right in the middle and there's no light anywhere. Or you could be just coming out and you see something glimmering down there at the end, but you're not sure if it's someone coming to help you or a freight train about to run you down.

"Ain't I EVER Gonna Get to the Top?"

Not long ago, while I was busy putting together a new issue of our newsletter, the phone rang. The voice on the other end belonged to a dear lady from deep in the heart of Mississippi. Her life was full of troubles—an abusive husband, the death of her child after suffering a long time with cancer, and she wasn't well herself.

She went on for several minutes about all her problems. Finally, she paused for breath and said, "Barbara, it just seems like I've been rockin' so long at the bottom . . . ain't I ever gonna get to the top?"

"Yes, of course, you will," I assured her. "God has brought you this far, and He will NEVER leave you. His comfort blanket is right there. Wrap yourself up in it and remember that NOTHING can separate you from the love of God. You WILL make it. You WILL survive, and you WILL find the light at the end of the tunnel. Certainly, one day you will look back on all your painful situations and be able to see how God used them to FINE-TUNE you for His glory, making you a golden treasure in His sight. All this has come to pass, not to stay. You hang on to Jesus real tight, and you won't stay at the bottom; you'll get OVER the top!"

We shared together for a few more minutes. I hadn't made her problems go away, but as she hung up she said she felt better. Talking it out had given her something to help keep her going.

Some people have said that my positive attitude is a put-on—that I'm really in denial, trying to escape reality. My answer is that there's no point in denying reality. In fact, I encourage folks who have been terribly hurt to go ahead and grieve because the Lord sometimes takes us into troubled waters, not to drown us, but to *cleanse* us. As we face our problems, however, it's perfectly okay to escape sometimes by looking for the humorous side of things. Tears begin your healing process, and laughter propels it along.

Folks often write to confirm my theory that humor heals. The other morning as I was working on this book, I received a brief letter from a fellow survivor who said:

> I must say that I admire your courage and sense of humor. I've always been told that if the Lord shuts one door, another will open. Well, I've been in a long hallway for

over two years, and since reading your book, I've exited this dark hallway and feel refreshed. Even the password on my computer now is "Freshstart"!

In this book I'd like to have you to join me in looking for laughter in the face of adversity. No matter where you are in the

Adapted from a cartoon by Sandy Ritz, R.N., Honolulu, Hawaii.
Used by permission.

tunnel (or, if you prefer, the parentheses), it dilutes your pain to see the humor in life. That's the way I have survived, and I know you can too.

And there is humor everywhere—from automobile bumpers (what I like to call "bumper snickers") to funny book titles you can find in supermarket aisles. While shopping recently, I came upon one titled:

BABIES AND OTHER HAZARDS OF SEX[3]

That didn't hit me as particularly funny, but then I came to the subtitle:

How to Make a Tiny Person in Nine Months
with Tools You Probably Have Around the House

I just lost it and had to hold on to my shopping cart to keep from collapsing with laughter right there in the aisle. A couple of nearby shoppers gave me strange looks, probably wondering if I had escaped from a nearby home for the bewildered, but I didn't care. I love to laugh, and I want to encourage you to laugh too. Maybe that's the real reason for the crazy title of this book—to provoke a REAL LAUGH, a genuine chuckle. If it's done that for you, then we've already started accomplishing our goal.

So bring your hammer if you like, or leave it back on the workbench; let's explore together how to gain hope and encouragement through the power of humor. As somebody said:

LAUGHTER IS LIKE PREMIUM GASOLINE:
IT HELPS TAKE THE KNOCK OUT OF LIVING!

The Head Thinks, the Hands Labor, But It's the Heart That Laughs*

Dear Barb,

I have not laughed so much in years. My husband and I have been married twelve years and we have two lovely girls. My medical history could fill a book! And through it all I'd forgotten what it felt like to have a deep, gut-filled laugh! It was so refreshing to me. I sing a lot and that helps, but your book brought me something I could never live without again—laughter.

- - - - - - -

I love what this lady says above about laughter being something she can't live without. I agree. Laughter is nutrition for your soul, a tourniquet to stop the bleeding of a broken heart, an encouraging tonic for the discouraged. We need to laugh for our physical, emotional, and spiritual health. Solomon knew this, and that's why he had this to say about laughter:

---

* For the title of this chapter, I am indebted to Liz Curtis Higgs, *An Encourager*®, P.O. Box 43577, Louisville, Kentucky 40253.

"A cheerful heart does good like medicine, but a broken spirit makes one sick" (Prov. 17:22 TLB).

Sometimes folks say my specialty is making people laugh, but that's not really my major goal. I use laughter to flatten out the pain folks feel because of the blows life has dealt them. And there is a lot of pain out there in Spatulaland.

It seems that everyone can use a good laugh, or even a chuckle. One lady wrote: "I'm fifty-nine years old. My husband and daughter died two years ago with cancer. My son was killed in 1984 in a skiing accident; he had just turned twenty-one. I take care of my eighty-year-old mother and my ninety-year-old father-in-law. Last year I had to go back to work to support them (and myself). You can see I do need a smile now and then . . ."

Another dear gal dropped me a line on a tiny three-by-five card that read, "Thanks for your humorous look at life, which threatens, at times, to beat us mothers into the ground! I don't have the same kind of problems you do, but it sure helps to be reminded to look at any problems with a prayer and laughter . . ."

Folks frequently send me cards with cute greetings, illustrations, and cartoons. One gal's card had a darling little teddy bear on the front wearing a big heart on his chest, and while she didn't quite have the title of *Geranium* right,[1] I got her message:

> Several years ago I read your *Daisy* book and laughed and cried until I couldn't wring out another tear. Since my husband was in the hospital at the time and very ill, your book brought to the surface the joy I always have in the Lord. I even read it to my husband, and he laughed too. Since then he has improved very much. God is so *good!* . . .

One of my favorite notes, however, didn't come in the mail, but was left on the windshield of my car (which has SPATULA license plates) while I was in a local market doing some grocery shopping:

Noon Thursday

   Barbara Johnson! I know you're here in one of these stores somewhere! Just wish I knew where and what you look like, so I could introduce myself and tell you how much joy you've brought to my life — — and laughter!

   I've enjoyed you so much every time I've heard you on the radio. You're such a delight!

   Since I live in La Habra and am frequently in the post office next to City Hall, I keep hoping I'll bump into you there. Or, at the very least, observe you getting a ticket for making another U-Turn in front of it !! ☺

   Gotta run — have to buy a colorful new GERANIUM for my hat!

        Love you,
        Carol Anne Posey

When You Hit Life's Potholes—Laugh

All the notes and letters quoted above are more proof that:

HUMOR IS TO LIFE WHAT
SHOCK ABSORBERS ARE TO AUTOMOBILES.[2]

   Life is full of bumps, potholes, and even washed-out bridges. So we need all the shock absorbers we can get! More doctors are agreeing that everyone needs to laugh more. In our tense, uptight society where folks are rushing to make appointments they have already missed, a good laugh can be as refreshing as a cup of cold water in the desert. The only way we can get through these devastating days is to look for humor, and in some cases, make our own fun times out of the disasters that could otherwise mess up our day.

For example, I recall the day when all the local papers carried stories about how some so-called experts thought the planets were supposed to line up and bring our world to an untimely end. That didn't happen, but the day did start out with Bill waking me out of a sound sleep at 6:00 A.M. to tell me the hot-water heater was LEAKING all over the place.

"I've got to get to work, but you must call the plumber IMMEDIATELY," Bill said as he dashed out the door to go to work.

It was awfully early to be calling a plumber, but I finally did get one to come over. One glance at our dripping water heater, and he announced it would have to be replaced—for three hundred dollars! Then he asked if I wanted a ten-year warranty or a five-year warranty. I replied that FIVE years would do fine because I didn't expect to be here any longer than THAT!

The plumber looked at me quizzically, then walked over to my kitchen table to fill out his work order. As usual, my table was loaded with tapes, books, mail, and other items, so he had to clear some space to write in his receipt book. And there, just two inches away, was a little paperback book someone had sent me, perhaps as a joke. The title blared out in big, purple letters: HOW TO BE A HAPPY HOMOSEXUAL! I had laid it there, thinking I would leaf through it later, and I know the plumber saw it.

He never said a word. He completed his paperwork, installed the new water heater, then left with a polite good-bye.

Later, as I was leaving for my daily run to the post office, I saw the book lying there on the table. I realized the plumber surely had gone home to tell his wife about this CRAZY lady who didn't plan to be around for any longer than five years. Not only that, but she was reading books like HOW TO BE A HAPPY HOMOSEXUAL! I began to laugh, and I laughed WILDLY all the way to the La Habra post office. All I could think about was how much FUN the poor guy would have, sharing his weird experiences on the day the world was supposed to have come to an end.

All things considered, you can see why I could use a good laugh.

Why Laughter Is Good for You

There are many articles and books about how healthy it is to laugh. On the physical side, laughter increases your breathing rate, which automatically increases the amount of oxygen in your blood, producing the aerobic effect usually associated with exercises like swimming and jogging.[3]

Laughter is good for your mental health too. I heard one expert suggest that we should learn to laugh at our embarrassing moments in life.[4] If we can't laugh about what has embarrassed us, we will remain embarrassed people. But if we can share our embarrassing moments with others, it achieves two things: first, we admit our imperfections, which helps other folks draw

closer to us; second, it's a great way to find things to laugh
about. For example, a special Spatula friend dropped me this
little note:

> I dashed in to the post office yesterday A.M. Went to put
> my keys in my pocket and discovered my shorts were on
> backwards! I left them like that all day and nobody even
> noticed. Actually, they felt pretty good, because my front
> is bigger than my behind!!!

Sometimes Feminine Protection Isn't

One of the funniest "most-embarrassing-moment" stories
I've come upon in a long time was about a lady who picked up
several items at a discount store. When she finally got up to the
checker, she learned that one of her items had no price tag.
Imagine her embarrassment when the checker got on the intercom and boomed out for all the store to hear: "PRICE CHECK
ON LANE THIRTEEN. TAMPAX. SUPER SIZE."

That was bad enough, but somebody at the rear of the store
apparently misunderstood the word "Tampax" for "THUMB-
TACKS." In a business-like tone, a voice boomed back over the
intercom: "DO YOU WANT THE KIND YOU PUSH IN WITH
YOUR THUMB OR THE KIND YOU POUND IN WITH A
HAMMER?"

This story, which was published in an unidentified newsletter
and sent to me by a friend, may make you smile, chuckle, or
possibly react with a little shock, but in that store at that moment,
everyone came unglued. Complete strangers held on to each
other to keep from collapsing as tears rolled down their faces.
The weary shoppers got an exhilarating lift from an unexpected
release of tension.

I'm sure the poor lady buying the Tampax was embarrassed,
but I hope that later she got a chuckle out of it, too, and could
share what happened with her friends. Laughing together over
life's little twists and turns is a great way to let off steam and
keep stress at a minimum.

A story I've been telling on myself recently concerns one of
my adventures while speaking in a church. Because the room

was a little stuffy, I asked that some water be left on the podium. Sure enough, when I got up to speak, there was a lovely embossed chalice full of water.

As I spoke I kept sipping from the goblet, and by the time I finished, ALL the water was gone. I appreciated that water SO much! Later, the conference hostess came up and apologized because she had forgotten to put the drinking water on the podium. She told me I had been drinking from a chalice of holy water the pastor used to baptize babies! At that point I had a choice: decide to be ill or decide it was funny. I laughed and said, "Really? Actually, it tasted pretty good!"

When you're willing to tell funny little personal stories on yourself, you'll have all kinds of fun. As comedian Victor Borge said:

THE SHORTEST DISTANCE BETWEEN TWO PEOPLE
IS A SMILE.[5]

Learn to Jump-Start Laughter

Some folks tell me, "But, Barbara, I'm not very good at laughing. Besides, I don't have a lot to laugh about right now."

I understand, but laughing is like a lot of things—if you want to be GOOD at it, you have to WORK at it. To start your day, try this simple exercise: Stand in front of the mirror, place your hands on your tummy, and laugh. Try for a "bottom-to-top" laugh that comes from deep in your belly. It's okay if you can only manage one big "HA!" at first. Then try a big "HA HA!" Keep adding more "HA's" until you've got your diaphragm going, and before you know it, the laughter will be rolling out of you.

This may sound a little crazy, but it works. You can literally jump-start yourself into having a good laugh just about any time you want to.

You may be wondering, "Does laughing really do all *this?*" Yes, it does if you will believe one thing:

WE DON'T LAUGH BECAUSE WE'RE HAPPY;
WE'RE HAPPY BECAUSE WE LAUGH.

Remember that just as you have different tastes in food and clothing, you have tastes in humor. Know what kind of humor appeals to you, and look for it in films, videos, cartoons, books, and magazines. Also, seek out people who make you laugh. It may be a certain friend, or one of your children, or a grand-child. Whoever it is, spend time with that person.

Do everything you can to cultivate a sense of humor, which involves more than just telling jokes. A sense of humor is con-nected to the way you look at life, the way you can chuckle over what is absurd and ridiculous, the way you put your prob-lems in perspective, and the way you can feel joy because you know that:

ANY DAY ABOVE GROUND IS A GOOD ONE!

Some folks know the meaning of this slogan in spades. One lady wrote to tell me she had just begun her climb out of a black hole of despair that started two years ago when her forty-year-old husband contracted lupus. After a while he lost his ability to walk, ending his hopes of becoming a coach.

Then their youngest son, a teenager, was found unconscious on the bathroom floor with his wrists cut and bleeding. He had tried to kill himself because he had been "hearing voices." Later, they learned the boy had gotten involved in Satanism through some friends he knew at school.

To cap everything off, this mom is having problems with two older children as well. One daughter doesn't want her for a mother anymore, and the other has just left her second hus-band. Despite ALL this, the woman wrote:

> About here I started my descent into the deep hole I had been slowly digging. I have always been good at digging holes, and now I had fallen in headfirst. I found myself sitting alone in the dark with my thoughts leading me deeper and deeper into hopelessness.
>
> I could not find comfort in my husband's gentle encour-agement, and I could not find my answer in God. I, too, was at the point of suicide when I finally went for help. I

have received some counseling, and while reading your book, sat there laughing and crying and wondering how I could do both. I think that is the whole point of your book. I am going to look for the joy in my circumstances. Many of those circumstances have not changed, but I am looking at them differently. I have turned my eyes back to my Lord. I KNOW He has the answers.

The "Earthquake" Left Us Shaking with Laughter

The more you look for humor, the more you'll find it. Try keeping a journal that notes the humorous things you've read, seen, or heard. Clip cartoons to put on your bulletin board or the family fridge. Share them with visitors and guests. You never know when you'll need something to add a little joy to your life.

We *all* needed something to brighten up our lives this year when the devastating earthquake struck Southern California. (They say it wasn't the "big one," but it was sure big enough for me!) One woman wrote to tell me how one little splash of joy reminded her to keep on smiling through her tears as she cleaned up her home after the quake. She wrote:

> About a year ago I attended a retreat where you were the speaker, and you gave each lady some sparkle stones to take home and put on a window sill. I did. Then I kind of forgot about them. But their message of Jesus' love came to me as I was cleaning a huge mess of broken things after the earthquake.
>
> The refrigerator and all the cupboards had opened and emptied, and everything had broken into millions of pieces. I was sad, scared, and upset as I cleaned. Then I saw a "sparkle" among my broken treasurers. I cried as I scooped up the little sparkle stone and thanked God that I had been able to have those treasures for the years I had enjoyed them. I thought, "for this I have Jesus." When I saw that sparkle stone I had to smile and say, "Thank you, Barbara, for this reminder that Jesus loves me. I'll sparkle for Him."

One of the funny things about humor is that some things are amusing to some people, but not to others. It's always fun to see what will get a laugh and what will not. Sometimes a lot depends on the atmosphere or the company you're in at the moment. For example, when my sister, Janet, and I get together we usually find lots to laugh at, sometimes by accident and sometimes just because we're both on a "wacko" wavelength.

A few years ago, after we had had another one of our more impressive Southern California earthquakes, Janet came out from Minnesota to visit us for a few days. Naturally, because of the recent shaker, which had been around 5.5 on the Richter scale, she was rather apprehensive. One morning Janet mentioned she wanted to put "a few things" in the washer. She didn't know that if the load is too light it tends to throw our washer off balance, and I hadn't paid any attention to the small number of items she intended to wash.

We were sitting at the kitchen table, chatting away while the washer made its usual whirring sounds in the nearby utility room. Suddenly we heard all kinds of *BOOMING* and *BUMP-ING* noises, then our entire mobile home began to *SHAKE*. Unaware of the improperly loaded washer, my first thought was *EARTHQUAKE!* "Get under the table *QUICK!*" I shouted to Janet. "And keep your head covered."

My big sister hadn't moved THAT fast for years! Come to think of it, I was moving pretty fast myself to get under the table WITH her when I suddenly suspected what was really wrong—the washer was just out of balance.

I staggered over to open the utility room door, and there was the washer, chugging along as usual after propelling itself to the next cycle. All the *BOOM-BOOM* and shaking had stopped, and I told Janet, "It's okay. It's not an earthquake. It's just the washer."

We looked at each other for a few seconds. Then Janet started to giggle. That got me going, and pretty soon we were both laughing hysterically (and with a great deal of relief). It was a good example of how close we all live to the ragged edge here in Southern California. Any time we feel any kind of shaking or trembling, we think, "IT'S THE BIG ONE!"

I can still remember the time a quake hit while two local TV newscasters were broadcasting. As the studio shook and the big lights overhead started swaying, their eyes grew wide and then the two men disappeared from sight. *From under their news desk,* they continued giving the story on the latest earthquake to hit the area!

Now I understand just how they felt. When an earthquake strikes, you'll dive under anything to protect yourself. Janet and I laughed most of the day about the "washer earthquake." What fun! I told her I'd have to try that again sometime when we had company over just to see if EVERYONE would run for shelter. It would be especially fun with out-of-state guests. Then they could say they lived through an earthquake.

The Hunchback of La Habra

Laughter has a way of being contagious, particularly when Janet and I get together. On another occasion when she was visiting, she helped me read through some mail, something I really appreciated because I'm always behind in that department. As we worked through one of the many stacks of letters, Janet came upon one that said:

> I love you Barbara for all you've done while on the earth. Maybe someday I'll be able to give you a big hug. But if I don't see you on this earth I'll see you in Heaven.
> I know I'll recognize you, you'll be the one with the hunched over back from the weight of your crown.

After reading the letter aloud to me, Janet started laughing. "Let me look at that," I told her. "I'm not sure I see what's so funny."

As I read the letter, I started to smile. Then I started to chuckle along with Janet. Before I knew it, we were in hysterics over the very thought of what this friend was saying. Later, Janet was trying to tell someone about it on the phone, and she began laughing so hard she couldn't get the words out.

It's hard to say why my friend's note struck us as being so funny. Perhaps it was the mental picture she created of me carrying that great big crown! Of course, we know we will all have

crowns in heaven. I like the Scripture that talks about blessings for those who persevere under trial, because when they have stood the test, they will receive "the crown of life that God has promised to those who love him."[6]

There is a song about having "stars in my crown," which I guess would be a special joy. But just being a daughter of the King and wearing a crown of glory that will never fade will be enough for me.

Yes, laughter CAN be contagious, not to mention unpredictable. As somebody said, perhaps laughter is the cheapest luxury we have. It stirs up the blood, expands the chest, electrifies the nerves, clears away the cobwebs from the brain, and gives the whole system a cleansing rehabilitation. A good laugh is the best medicine, whether you are sick or not. In fact:

LAUGHTER IS TO LIFE
WHAT SALT IS TO AN EGG.

Because we can never get enough laughter, I've decided to devote the rest of this chapter to humorous things folks have sent me. Some of them have appeared in our newsletter, but others have not. You'll find all kinds of humor, from bloopers and malapropisms to crazy stories I've collected through the years. Out of this potpourri of humor, I'm sure you'll get some chuckles and maybe even a belly laugh. By the way, did you know that another name for a belly laugh is a *MIRTHQUAKE?*

Accident Reports Can Be a Crackup

I love collecting the funny things people say in accident-insurance reports. Here's one of the best lists I've found:

- Coming home I drove into the wrong house and collided with a tree I don't have.
- The guy was all over the road. I had to swerve a number of times before I hit him.

- I was on my way to the doctor with rear-end trouble when my universal joint gave way, causing me to have an accident.

- I was thrown from my car as it left the road. I was later found in a ditch by some stray cows.

- I told the police I was not injured but upon removing my hat, found that I had a fractured skull.

- The indirect cause of the accident was a little guy in a small car with a big mouth.

- In order to avoid a collision, I ran into the other car.

- The accident was entirely due to the road bending.[7]

A Short Sermon Designed for Prime Time

Television programs are supposed to entertain us, and sometimes they even succeed. Recently I was sent the following item by Roger Shouse, a pastor friend of mine in the Midwest. Roger wrote this "Guide to the TV Guide" himself, and I hope you find it as fun and thought-provoking as I did:

> GOOD MORNING AMERICA. TODAY is full of new hope and optimism in THE DAYS OF OUR LIVES. Each 60 MINUTES of this day can be used to further our journey on the HIGHWAY TO HEAVEN. AS THE WORLD TURNS in its self-seeking interests, we as Christians must realize that we live in ANOTHER WORLD. When we remember that Jesus died for our sins, THE PRICE IS RIGHT, then, for God to call us "ALL MY CHILDREN."
>
> But sometimes, IN THE HEAT OF THE NIGHT, THE YOUNG AND THE RESTLESS, amid GROWING PAINS, will forget these eternal truths and act like PERFECT STRANGERS to their God. In so doing, they fail to acknowledge WHO'S THE BOSS and become a real WISEGUY in their own eyes.
>
> Acting this way not only puts one's soul in JEOPARDY with God, but it hurts the family as well. Without God's truths directing us, FAMILY FEUDs wind up in DIVORCE COURT. Whether we live in DALLAS or L.A., LAW is still

law with God. We must let Jesus be the king of our lives (1 Pet. 3:15). And whether you are *THIRTYSOMETHING* or one of *THE GOLDEN GIRLS* you will surely be *THE BOLD AND THE BEAUTIFUL* to God when you walk with Him each day of your life.

We have but *ONE LIFE TO LIVE*. And instead of chasing the world and all its *DESIGNING WOMEN*, we ought rather to follow *THE GUIDING LIGHT* of Jesus Christ.

Indeed, this is a good day—enjoy it to the fullest, making the most of your opportunities, for someday we shall all stand before *THE JUDGE*.[8]

Every Little Joy Helps

It's obvious this chapter could keep right on going to become a book of its own, so maybe it's time to stop with just a few short items that I hope contain a splash of joy. First, here is how one of my friends makes her favorite casserole:

My favorite casserole recipe: Combine everything from the left side of the fridge. Put potato chips on top. Bake.

From Liz Curtis Higgs, *Does Dinner in a Bucket Count?* (Nashville: Thomas Nelson, 1992), 71. Drawing by Carol Cornette. Used by permission.

Recipes like this are why Bill often says, "Barbara cooks for fun, but for FOOD, we go out." He also tells everyone that if he wants to hide something from me, he puts it in the oven. He knows I'll NEVER find it there!

Why do I work so hard at helping people laugh? The other day a lady dropped me a note that says it all:

> I am sure you have had numerous tales of woe sent to you. I won't bother you with mine, but your books and talks have prepared me for the disaster I am now living. Every little joy helps. Thanks for loving others so richly.

My friend is right: *every little joy DOES help*. Laughter may not necessarily get you out of your tunnel, but it will definitely light your way. Remember:

> *Laughter is like changing a baby's diaper:*
> *It doesn't permanently solve any problems,*
> *but it makes things more acceptable for a while.*

*Bugaboo Busters**

As the guest checked out of the plush hotel, he noticed a sign on the door of his room: "Have you left anything?"

As he paid his bill at the front desk, the traveler informed the manager, "Your sign is wrong. It should say, 'Have you anything left?'"[9]

---

* Recently, when someone was telling me about the terrible situation her family was in because of a wayward child, I sympathized by telling her she was in "a real bugaboo." As soon as I said it I realized it was exactly the right term to describe this book's chapter-ending collections of joy-filled pain-smashers: *Bugaboo Busters!* I hope you'll agree it's perfect for a book with a crazy title like *Mama, Get the Hammer! There's a Fly on Papa's Head!*

HAVING A GREAT AIM IS IMPORTANT . . .
SO IS KNOWING WHEN TO PULL THE TRIGGER.

Thanksgiving riddle:
Why do the Pilgrims' pants keep falling down?
BECAUSE THEY WEAR THEIR BELTS
AROUND THEIR HATS!

Bumper Snicker Sightings:
BE CAREFUL: I DRIVE THE SAME WAY YOU DO!
I STILL MISS MY EX-HUSBAND,
BUT MY AIM IS GETTING BETTER.[10]
CHEER UP!
SOMEDAY YOU'LL BE DEAD.[11]

Life is full of uncertainties . . .
(or could I be wrong about that?)
Ashleigh Brilliant, Pot-shot
4241, © 1987.

A SMILE IS THE LIGHT IN THE WINDOW OF YOUR FACE
THAT TELLS PEOPLE YOU'RE AT HOME.

I'M NOT SPOILED . . .
I'M NOT.
I'm not . . .
i'm not . . . i'm not . . .[12]

Updated Witticisms
LIGHTNING NEVER STRIKES TWICE,
BUT ISN'T ONCE ENOUGH?

A BIRD IN THE HAND
WILL POOP IN YOUR PALM.

SILENCE IS DARNED HARD TO COME BY
WHEN YOU HAVE KIDS.[13]

I HAVE SEEN THE TRUTH,
AND IT MAKES NO SENSE.[14]

If you can smile when things go wrong,
you have someone else in mind to blame.[15]

Medical Confusion to Tickle the Funny Bone

Some of the more peculiar ailments described by patients to their doctors include: "Migrating" headaches, "Prospect" glands, "Mental" pause, "Scat cans" of the brain.

One man mentioned that someone quit breathing and had to have "artificial insemination." One woman requested a "monogram." Another complained of pain in the "palms of my feet." Still another told the doctor before her operation: "Don't worry. If anything happens, my son has the power of eternity."[16]

When a woman is gloomy, everything seems to go wrong; when she is cheerful, everything seems right. (Prov. 15:15 TLB)[17]

Some Days You're the Pigeon, Some Days You're the Statue[*]

*W*hen I ran across this cute saying about pigeons and statues, I thought, *What a perfect description of the stress that is part of our daily lives.*

When you have life's pressures under control, you're like a pigeon who soars high above the problems. But when life drops a load of stress on you, you come out all covered with doo-doo.

When that happens, there are several responses you can make:

• You can be as stoic as a statue or you can throw a pity party, complaining loudly that life is for the birds. Use either of these negative approaches and the stress will wear you down, defeat you, and possibly make you sick.

• You can accept what's happening and maintain a positive attitude at the same time. One of the best ways to cope with stress is to grasp an all-important concept:

---

[*] For the title of this chapter I am indebted to Dr. Roger Andersen, *Some Days You're the Pigeon, Some Days You're the Statue: Comic Confessions of a College Professor* (Sarasota Springs, N.Y.: The Humor Project, 1993).

LAUGHTER AND LEARNING GO HAND-IN-HAND.

When you're able to take your bloopers, boo-boos, or blunders and see the humor in the situation, you reduce your stress and turn it into a POSITIVE force that will help you grow and WIN. One mom wrote to tell me that she just screwed up the courage to contact the judge who had sentenced her son, not to ask for any favors, but to let him know that it hurt to have her boy gone, and she wanted to reach out in love to other young people to keep them out of trouble. Her letter continued:

> I have had some trouble sleeping alone in our country home, even though I asked the Lord to protect me. Last night at our family Bible study we were talking about the different translations of the Bible and I started to laugh. When the others wanted me to share what was so funny, I told them that I had solved the problem of being alone. I would just take King James to bed with me. I did just that and I slept all night, it was a simple thing but it was just what I needed.

Our High School Was Special

The tragedies that hit our family brought all kinds of stress. Perhaps one reason I have been able to overcome major stress in adult life is that I learned how to handle stress when I was younger, especially during my teenage years.

When my father died, World War II was in full swing and Mom had to work teaching music. Janet had married and I was just entering high school. A family friend wanted to help out, so he offered to send me to a private Christian high school in the Deep South, many miles from my hometown. It was a well-respected institution, and being allowed to even go there was a real honor.

When I arrived at the school, the first thing I saw was a huge sign over the inside of the front door of the dormitory:

GRIPING NOT TOLERATED

I didn't know what the sign meant because in our family "griping" meant throwing up! This was the first of many misunderstandings I would have at this school.

Later I saw that there were big signs over the doors of ALL rooms in the school. One simply said, DO RIGHT. Another one stated, DON'T SACRIFICE THE PERMANENT ON THE ALTAR OF THE IMMEDIATE. And still another sign I remember warned, PEOPLE WHO PUT OFF LITTLE THINGS NEVER PUT OVER BIG THINGS. To put it mildly, in this institution, signs were a BIG part of life.

On my very first night, the teachers called a meeting to inform the new students about THE RULES. We each got a handbook detailing every rule and explaining the number of demerits that would be given for any infractions. As we went over the rules during the meeting, we learned that demerits were given for being late for a meal or for class. Demerits were given for singing "Happy Birthday" to someone if it wasn't REALLY his or her birthday. And you could receive demerits for not having your feet ON THE FLOOR when the rising bell rang or for having a light on after 10:30 P.M.

Discipline was meted out according to how many demerits you received for breaking THE RULES. If you accumulated 150 demerits during any one semester, you were shipped home in disgrace. Your trunk would be hauled into the front of the chapel so the entire student body could see your name on your trunk and know you had been expelled.

Every Friday night typewritten lists were posted in the dormitories with the names of those who had received demerits during the week. If your name was there, you had to go before the DISCIPLINE COMMITTEE to explain the circumstances. If you had a reasonable explanation, it might be possible to have the demerits removed, but otherwise they STAYED on your record. Most infractions of the rules only gained you five or ten demerits. So it would take a LOT to accumulate the 150 that would mean being shipped home.

There was one rule, however, that carried a HUGE demerit fine, and it almost led to my early exit. Among the signs that were posted all over the school, there was one identical sign in every room: NO COOKING IN YOUR ROOM. I thought that was a peculiar rule. Who would want to COOK in her room? Besides, we didn't have any hot plates anyway.

But after a few weeks of eating in the dining hall, which featured hominy grits, black-eyed peas, and something that looked like boiled mothballs, I was desperate for some REAL FOOD. My roommate and I worked in the dining room as waitresses, and one night we pilfered some bread and cheese and brought it to our room where we decided to make grilled-cheese sandwiches. But what could we use to grill them? We slipped downstairs to the laundry room and brought back two irons!

Using a little Noxzema face cream for grease, we put the cheese between the bread and then pressed the sandwiches between the irons. Soon we were enjoying what we thought were fantastic grilled-cheese sandwiches, Noxzema face cream and all!

As we munched on our sandwiches, the hall monitor knocked at our door. Some seniors who lived down the hall had smelled the grilling cheese and had turned us in.

Not only did we not know that the older students had been instructed to report rule violations by new students, but even worse, we had no idea that the penalty for breaking the rule of NO COOKING IN THE ROOM was 149 demerits!

During our hearing before the Discipline Committee, they somehow overlooked the fact that we had pilfered the sandwich ingredients from the kitchen and that we had nearly ruined two irons. We were given a strict warning that we both had to get through the entire semester with NO MORE DEMERITS. If we got even ONE MORE, we would be shipped home.

Talk about STRESS! Believe me, when you've only got one demerit left, you stay on your toes. I got up extra early to get my room cleaned and to get to class on time. And I scrupulously obeyed the school's prize rule, which was posted all over the place: GRIPING NOT TOLERATED.

Demerits were handed out on pink slips that were usually passed out during mealtime every day of that semester. Believe me, I sweated out avoiding those pink slips! Many years before Johnny Cash made the song, "I Walked the Line," popular, I learned the full meaning of the term. Somehow I survived the rest of the semester without getting one more demerit.

On one occasion my roommate and I were walking down the hall to check the bulletin board to see who got demerits. Just for fun, we were singing the hymn, "Is my name written there . . . on the page bright and fair?" We began laughing—until we remembered we could get demerits for *just singing in the hall*, not to mention making fun of the demerit list!

The point to this little story is there were two ways I could have reacted to the stress of having to obey all those rules and living a "perfect life" for several months without a hitch. I could have just said, "Forget it. This place is for the birds. I'd rather go home anyway." Undoubtedly, I would have been gone at once.

Instead, fear motivated me to do everything I could to cooperate. Actually, there was a GOOD side to all the rules. Before going to this school, I was like most teenagers and did my share of griping. But when I went on probation, I learned a whole new way to react. When you go through a whole semester consciously telling yourself, "I will not gripe," it helps you gain a different kind of attitude. In fact, it becomes a POSITIVE habit.

As I look back on my high school days, I can see that some of the rules seemed silly, but the overall result was good. I learned to be a positive person, which has helped me deal with stress all my life.

Stress Won't Go Away, So . . .

So far, I have received over fifty letters from people who say reading one of my books was the difference between life and death. I especially like this one:

> Oh, what a joy you have been! You truly saved my life! I hadn't heard of or read any of your work. Then my pastor's wife loaned me *Geranium*. . . . My first thought

was, *Oh, perfect, just what I need—another help book.* But yours really worked! I had spent most of my time feeling like an aerosol can—PRESSURIZED. Even though my problems are still there, it is a little easier to cope now. If you can get through the horrible problems you had, I'm sure I will too.

As this lady says so well, stress saps your energy and draws out all the bounce you need just for daily living. What can you do? The trick is not in asking God to get rid of the stress, but to learn how to cope with it to neutralize its effect. We are all in stressful situations, and the best approach is to accept and deal with them rather than fuss and fret, which only causes added

And You think there's stress in your life!

tension. Instead of being statues, we can be pigeons, soaring high above all the hassle.

Sometimes, however, it's hard to soar with the pigeons because of all the *turkeys* in your life. Plenty of folks who write to Spatula have been in the statue category. It's always good to hear from someone who survived incredible stress and still was able to fly high later on.

One gal wrote with an unbelievable story that began happily as she grew up in a warm loving church where she was always "the good kid." After a year of Bible college, she married a man she thought was a Christian, but for several years he mentally and physically abused her, as well as threatening their three beautiful children. Finally, after the husband shot the family cat, smashed up the house, and pulled a gun on her, she took her kids and left, then called the police. Not long after, she filed for divorce.

Later she met a truly nice Christian man; they were married and he adopted her three kids. Life seemed good again, but a few months later the doctors told her that her six-year-old son had cancer. They didn't expect the boy to live more than two or three months.

This mom went through it all, staying at the hospital with her son for three weeks, night and day, hating God, cursing God, and screaming, "Why my little boy? Why not some wino or drug addict or abused child that would be better off dead? Why my perfect, loving, up-till-now healthy child?"

Her son started weekly chemo treatments, monthly spinal taps, and bone marrow treatments that continued a total of four years. During this time, Mom wasn't well herself—then she learned she was pregnant!

"God did give us a perfect little girl during this time of hell," she wrote. "I guess it was then that I began to forgive Him."

Her daughter was born whole and healthy, but just a few months later the mother was in a car accident that left her partially crippled. When this injury finally began to heal, she started having abnormal Pap smears and wound up having a hysterectomy at the age of thirty-three.

But she didn't give up. She got back to work by starting her own at-home typing service so she could be around when her kids needed her but still bring in an income. Things are still tight because her husband has been laid off, but through it ALL, this mom has remained positive in the face of repeated disappointments. Her letter concludes:

> I have forgiven God, and a lot of good things and friends have come our way since our son's diagnosis. He beat the cancer, and continues to baffle the doctors to this day. I am healthier now than I ever was, and our family is binding and building. We're closer now than ever. One heartache after another, but now I can sing again for the first time in twelve years. . . .

The Difference between Winning and Losing

Wow! Just reading this last letter is stressful, but the best part is that this lady comes up a WINNER. Winners turn stress into something good; losers let stress turn life into something bad. Winners see an answer for every problem; losers see a problem for every answer.

The difference between winning and losing is how we choose to react to disappointments. We all have felt the pangs of disappointment at some time. Some of us remember in living color the day a spouse walked out or a child left home to go into a rebellious lifestyle. Others have felt the twisting knife of grief when a loved one dies, and many know the sinking feeling after hearing the doctor say, "I'm sorry. It's malignant."

The sharp sting of disappointment also comes with the frustration of being misunderstood by your family or at your job. And then there is the rejection of losing that job. The day after buying one of my books a woman was called into her supervisor's office and told that the department she had headed for eight years was being eliminated and that her staff would now report to a young man who had been with the company only six months. She wrote:

In other words, I was to begin looking for another job. I really felt bad, and I mean BAD! I'm a woman over forty without an MBA hanging from my neck, but I worked very hard all my life, and I'm very good at what I do. I had an idea of what was coming because the company philosophy as of late has been to replace the middle-aged management staff with new MBA blood, so when I was called into the meeting where I would later be fired, the first thing I saw was your book on my desk. I grabbed a pad and wrote with a purple highlighter "Pain Is Inevitable But Misery Is Optional!" I took the pad with me into the meeting and continued to glance at the words and repeated them in my head. It was the only thing that helped me keep my place and my dignity through what I considered one of the most humiliating moments of my life.

For most of us, it does, indeed, seem that pain is inevitable. From the necessity of labor pains to the inevitability of death, adversity is an integral part of life. Years ago I found a saying that not only helps me accept adversity, but even welcome it:

THE IRON CROWN OF SUFFERING
PRECEDES THE GOLDEN CROWN OF GLORY.

Some folks think life should always blow with a gentle breeze, and they whine if things don't go their way. If the currents against them are too strong, they throw up their hands and say, "Nothing ever goes right for me!"

The apostle Paul knew something about disappointment. The rejection, beatings, and imprisonments he endured made him an expert in living with stress. But Paul knew his God would never forsake him. He wrote:

WE ARE HARD PRESSED ON EVERY SIDE,
BUT NOT CRUSHED;
PERPLEXED, BUT NOT IN DESPAIR;
PERSECUTED, BUT NOT ABANDONED;
STRUCK DOWN, BUT NOT DESTROYED.[1]

Paul's life was proof that we can be victors rather than victims. You may remember a woman named Anna Mary Robertson. She married Tom Moses and had ten children. When Anna Mary got older, she was plagued with arthritis in her hands. At the age of eighty, she was looking for a pastime and took up painting because she found the paintbrush easy to hold. Today we know her as Grandma Moses, a gifted artist who painted more than fifteen hundred sought-after paintings. Twenty-five percent of her paintings were done after she was one hundred years old!

Examples like this are everywhere. Though we face disappointment, we can choose how we react. We can look for strength from God as we draw upon the companionship of Christ. Paul knew that even though there would be adversity, Christ was with him and would never leave him nor negate him. Christ would be there—forgiving, reconciling, making all things new. Whatever Paul was lacking, Jesus filled in the gaps.

The same can be true for you and me. Pain is inevitable, but misery, indeed, is optional. Adversity will come. The winds of adversity will sting your face. The storms of life will almost bury you. But . . .

BE BRAVE.
REMEMBER: THE WORST THAT CAN HAPPEN
IS THE WORST THAT CAN HAPPEN.
Ashleigh Brilliant Pot-shot #301 © 1971.

No matter what kind of stress threatens to overwhelm you, you can survive and be a winner. As somebody said, "Hallelujah, we win! I read the back of the book, and WE WIN!"

God will never let you sink under your circumstances. He ALWAYS provides a safety net. His love always encircles you.

Above all, God always keeps His promises! Whatever the stress you're facing right now, you WILL get through it. You will win, and after you're a winner, you can reach back and help along another suffering, stressed-out person who needs to hear the good news that she can be a winner, too!

Do You Ever Take Time for You?

When life becomes more than you can handle, here's good advice:

Want a surefire way to deal with stress?
PAMPER YOURSELF!

Unfortunately, I have a hard time convincing some folks that it's okay to be good to yourself now and then. They have heard (some of them all their lives): "You must always be self-LESS, always concerned for others, NEVER thinking of yourself."

I'm all for being good to others. As we refresh others, we ourselves are refreshed (see Prov. 11:25). Jesus taught "It is more blessed to give than to receive" (Acts 20:35 NIV). But Jesus also taught us by example to get out of the rat race and recharge our batteries.

Jesus took time to enjoy Himself with others. He could have spent twenty-four hours a day healing the sick or teaching the multitudes, but you never see Jesus being pressured or stressed. The idea that you should never take time for yourself isn't biblical. In fact, it's a good way to disintegrate.

When frustrations develop into problems to stress you out, the best way to cope is to stop, catch your breath, and do something nice for yourself, not out of selfishness, but out of wisdom. YOU ARE NOT SUPERWOMAN. All of us need our batteries recharged, probably a lot more often than we want to admit. Remember:

EVERYONE NEEDS TO RENEW, RECHARGE . . .
AND RELAX.[2]

One of my special friends is Mary Lou, who has been struggling with us in Spatula for several years. When she first joined us, she was so far out you couldn't even get a RADAR fix on her. But she has come a long way with her marvelous sense of humor and, as we have laughed and cried together, I have learned a lot from her about coping with stress.

The other day Mary Lou told me that when she really feels down, she has a special way of being lifted. I was expecting some kind of spiritual gem, but instead she said, "I get out a video of an old Shirley Temple movie, put it on my tape player, grab a box of chocolate-chip cookies, and lie down for a couple of hours to ESCAPE it all!"

Memories Are Made of This

Mary Lou's routine reminds me that nostalgia can do a lot to help you relax. What are special memories of your childhood? If you asked our sons what they remembered, their first answer would be "fresh-popped popcorn." The fragrance of popping corn would permeate the house as Bill would regularly make huge bowls of it. (This was before the days of automatic poppers or microwave popcorn.) Bill just poured the corn into a big frying pan on the stove and shook it vigorously. The smell was even better than what you find in movie theaters, and the house was filled with that wonderful aroma.

When I think of the smells that made my childhood special, I remember running home for lunch rather than eating in the school cafeteria because we lived only three blocks away. The winter days in Michigan were cold and blustery, and I can still feel the crunch of the snow under my galoshes as I hurried home, often with the cold wind biting my face and my "babushka" getting all snowy as I made my way through the drifts. (Do you remember babushkas? We tied them around our heads like huge bandannas, and the more fringe they had on the edges, the better.)

I'd run up the steps into our house, and as I came through the door, I'd smell that wonderful homemade tomato soup, made with my mother's special chili sauce, which she had canned the summer before. Mom's sauce was so thick that it would be the equal of what people call salsa today. Mom always made a lot of it, canning it in the old glass Kerr jars and then storing it in the root cellar.

That sauce was her own special blend, and along with onions, peppers, and tomatoes, of course, it made her soup unforgettable. How I'd love to come in out of the biting cold wind into that warm house and stand over the floor register, feeling the heat flow up around me. And then I'd sit down to a bowl of that steaming hot tomato soup. What a delight! It was worth the freezing hike home just to SMELL that delicious soup.

Life Is Still "Mmmm, Mmmm, Good"

Although I moved to California many years ago and the freezing cold of Michigan winters is only a dim memory, I still vividly recall my Mom's tomato soup. Every now and then when I want to treat myself, I will make a special pot of soup. Sometimes it's tomato, but I also like split pea or vegetable. If I'm in a hurry, I just take out a "cup of soup" from a package, add hot water and stir. Whenever I drink soup, I use a special cup a friend gave me. It has pictures of the little Campbell Soup kids on it, along with the words: "MMMM, MMMM, GOOD."

Naturally, I make special preparations to enjoy my soup completely. First, if it's winter, I'll turn down the thermostat a little bit so it gets a little cool in the house. If it's summer, I'll turn up the air conditioner to make it cooler in the house and at least get the feeling of being a bit chilly. There's something about sipping soup when it's eighty degrees that isn't quite the same.

Next, I'll turn on my electric fireplace and pop a Gaither music tape in my VCR. Then I'll tip back in my La-Z-Boy chair and tuck myself in with a fluffy afghan (or my "quillow"—see chapter 7). Whatever I use, I'm always careful to tuck it in nice and snugly around my feet, because you can't feel cozy in an afghan or a quillow unless it's tucked *snugly* over your toes like a soft comfort blanket.

Then I just relax, listen to the music, sip my soup, and nurture myself. Oh, yes, I'm always sure to unplug the phone so I can have a few uninterrupted minutes to drink in the warmth of that comforting soup. It brings back the rich memories I have of those days as a child when I ran home from school and enjoyed Mom's tomato soup.

Sometimes for variety, I'll substitute hot cocoa in place of soup. To be truthful, it's probably hard to say which I really like better. To feel really luxurious, I may add a BIG dollop of Cool-Whip.

You may want to try giving yourself this kind of comfort break. Fix yourself some soup or cocoa. Be sure you have that nice fleecy comforter tucked around your feet. This is mandatory to capture that nurturing feeling. Then, sit back and relish those moments as you feel your energy flowing back. Your mood will literally rise from the bottom right up to the top.

It's amazing how a small pleasure like soup or cocoa can accomplish all this, but be sure you add those other important features: the comforter, the music, the stillness, and the aroma. They all magically blend together to make it a real time of renewal. You can literally feel the stress drain out of your body. Try it, you'll love it!

Sometimes I use Mary Lou's approach and rent an old movie. I pop it into the VCR, curl up in my La-Z-Boy recliner, pull my afghan or quillow around me, and lose my troubles in that glamorous romantic world of the black-and-white films of the forties and fifties. Unlike many of the films today, which only amplify the difficulties in life, these old movies play up the positive. In fact, films of yesteryear have HAPPY endings and reassure us that, no matter how awful things may seem, YOU CAN WORK IT OUT.

The number of old black-and-white classics is almost unlimited. I've enjoyed *Now, Voyager, The Philadelphia Story,* and *Mr. Smith Goes to Washington.* Sometimes you can find real bargains on videos in the discount stores. The other day I was in Wal-Mart and came across a package of three videos of *Our Gang,* priced at only nine dollars for the set. Years ago I would often sit with my boys to watch the antics of the Little Rascals, the main characters in the *Our Gang* movies. So you can see why I had to have those three videos! I took them home and had a video feast, garnished with precious memories and topped off with hot cocoa and Cool-Whip. It was a wonderful three hours, which reminded me of Bonnie Prudden's statement:

YOU CAN'T TURN BACK THE CLOCK,
BUT YOU CAN WIND IT UP AGAIN.

Use All of God's Armor—Plus a Stress Sack

While it's comforting to look forward to eternity we have to cope with the present, and we need all the help we can get to deal with stress. There is a wonderful passage in Paul's letter to the Ephesians that contains good advice for resisting the enemy whenever he attacks. If we want to be standing when it's all over, we need to put on ALL of the armor of God to cope with the fiery darts of stress that come from every direction.[3]

Do you know what a Christian streaker is? That's someone who puts on *only* the helmet of salvation! We also need the belt of truth, the breastplate of righteousness, the shoes of readiness to share God's peace, and the shield of faith. And, above all, we need always to trust in God through prayer.

There is a true story that concerns an elderly woman who had a great love for Psalm 91, especially the fourth verse, which reads, "He will cover you with His pinions, / And under His wings you may seek refuge" (NASB). *Pinions* are bird's feathers. When trouble arises, the woman always says to herself, "I am covered with feathers. I am covered with feathers."

One evening the woman was walking down a dark street and realized that she was being followed by two men. They came up on both sides of her in a menacing way. Following her devotional practice, she began praying loudly, "I am covered with feathers. I am covered with feathers."

One of the would-be muggers said to the other, "Hey, man, this woman is crazy! Let's get out of here!" And the men fled without taking her purse.[4]

Yes, God's armor can get you through all kinds of stress, but there's one more piece of equipment that I have just discovered.

It's called a STRESS SACK. I think every stress sack should be personal, and that's why I made up my own list of items to put in it. I keep my stress sack handy to remind me of ways to relax in the Lord, enjoy life, and apply, in a practical sense, crucial ideals such as truth, faith, and righteousness:

- A SMALL BOTTLE to remind me that God has collected all my tears—He knows all about me (see Ps. 56:8).

- ADHESIVE TAPE to remind me that a heart that's broken can be mended with God's healing love.

- A SMALL PAIR OF SCISSORS to cut out all the unnecessary stuff in my schedule that is causing a lot of my stress in the first place.

- A HANDKERCHIEF to remind me to dry someone's tears with a word, a note, or a hug.

- A FAVORITE BUMPER STICKER or greeting card to remind me to laugh—often.

- A PIECE OF CHALK to use when something unpleasant happens, so I can "chalk it up" to experience.

- A SMALL PEBBLE to remind me God is my rock.

- A NAIL to remind me that Jesus coped with some pretty heavy stress too.

- A THUMBTACK to remind me not to just sit on my problems.

- A SPATULA to remind me there is always someone else who needs love and help to be peeled off that ceiling.

That's my list of items; you may want to think of others for your own stress sack. The important thing is to choose the ones that work for you. And when you think *you've* got it bad, try not

to wallow in the "poor-me" cesspool too long. As one of my
sons told me recently:

COME DOWN OFF THAT CROSS—
WE NEED THE WOOD!

Bugaboo Busters

INTO EACH LIFE A LITTLE RAIN MUST FALL . . .
BUT WE COULD USE A LITTLE LESS SNOW.[5]

I've learned to accept birth and death,
but sometimes I still worry about what lies between.
> Ashleigh Brilliant, Pot-shot #92,
> © 1968.

THERE'S A WONDERFUL METHOD OF RELIEVING
FATIGUE CAUSED BY OVERWORK:
IT'S CALLED "REST."
> Ashleigh Brilliant, Pot-shot
> #2140, © 1981.

When things go bad, cheer up; remember, they
could always be worse. And, of course, if they do get
worse, it will make your heart smile to remember that
when it's this bad, it has to get better soon.

STILL WATER RUNS DEEP
WHEN THE TOILET OVERFLOWS.[6]

It is advantageous for us to have big crosses for they teach us to bear little ones calmly.

I TRIED RELAXING, BUT I DON'T KNOW . . .
I FEEL MORE COMFORTABLE BEING TENSE.

God will never lead you where His strength cannot keep you.

See! I will not forget you. . . . I have carved you on the palm of my hand. (Isa. 49:16)[7]

3

I Know a Little Suffering Is Good for the Soul, But Somebody Must Be Trying to Make a Saint Out of Me!

A darling mom who is part of one of our support groups once told me, "Spatula Ministries is a very elite bunch. It is a club where not many are willing to pay the initiation fee to become a member!"

She smiled when she said it, and I smiled back, knowing she was right. The initiation fee to become a "Spatulander" is suffering. Sooner or later, we all wind up with our "grief work" to do.

Understanding grief is a complicated process. Why do some folks recover after suffering a terrible loss, while others do not? Those who get better *have done their grief work*; those who don't go into a kind of denial—denying it happened, not willing to face the heartache of working through the grief period.

Grief work is never easy, never fun. But eventually we learn that no matter how bad the pain might be at a certain moment, we WILL function again—and even LAUGH again. We will realize that God has not forgotten us and we will hear Him say, "I know the plans I have for you. . . . They are plans for good and not for evil, to give you a future and a hope" (Jer. 29:11 TLB).

Denial Is Not a River in Egypt

If you're going to survive any trauma, the first thing to do is face it. When reality becomes too painful, we often try to flee to a never-never land called DENIAL, which is not a river in Egypt! Instead, denial is like a mirage in the desert. As psychotherapist Karl Jung said,

ALL NEUROSIS IS A SUBSTITUTE FOR
LEGITIMATE SUFFERING.

There is no way around suffering. We have to go through it to get to the other side. We cannot deny the impact of the *WHAMMEE* that has hit us. Many folks deny their pain. They try to bury themselves by escaping everyone and everything. Or they look for distractions that will help them numb their feelings. They deny their real emotions, thinking this NUMB-NESS will be a way to escape from their hurts.

But all this denial doesn't help you feel better. The grief process is like a life raft, and if you deny your grief it's like jumping off the raft into a school of hungry sharks. If you don't face your grief and work it through, it will eat you alive. This mom's letter puts it all in perspective:

> This month is a celebration of sorts . . . but let me explain:
>
> 1. I'm alive and well. The back pains have diminished.
> 2. The black cloud lifted quite some time ago. I make sure that I cry when I feel the need. Keeping "cried up" keeps your body healthy . . . the red eyes only last a little while.
> 3. I can navigate many miles beyond my house, now that I no longer feel the world closing in on me.
> 4. It was exactly a year ago my only child told me, "Mom, I'm a lesbian."
>
> I listed the above in reverse order because all of us who are slugging through the "slough of despondency" need to know again and again and again . . . that the darkest days can and will turn into brighter times.

Adapted from Ashleigh Brilliant, Pot-shot #2323 © 1981.

Real Folks DO Cry

Grief always starts with SHOCK. A loved one or a good friend dies, and we say, "Oh, no, not Mary!" We want to deny the pain, but we cannot heal what we cannot feel. So, Rule Number 1 is to stop saying, "I am NOT in pain." You ARE in pain, and the pain causes feelings of anger, guilt, and regret. It all adds up to grief. Instead of denying this, face it head-on and admit you are experiencing pain. *The sooner you deal with feeling your pain, the sooner it will pass.*

There is no timetable on grief work. Your grief time depends on the voltage of the relationship you had with the person you lost, or the importance of the dream that was not fulfilled. Go ahead and grieve your broken dreams. Grieve the expectations that were not met by that child who has disappointed you so dreadfully. Grieve whatever failures you think you are guilty of. We have numerous reasons to feel inadequate, but there is good news: *We do not have to be perfect to receive God's love and forgiveness.*

My best advice for grieving folks is something that may sound contradictory, but it has worked for me—many times:

TO SURVIVE, STAY IN THE PAIN.

In other words, allow yourself to experience your emotions. Deal with your anxiety, depression, or anger by being willing to reach out for help. Shame-based folks don't feel they have the right to ask for help. Here is an opportunity to let someone love you. Be powerless and let others help. There is a great healing in this.

Women can almost always "stay in the pain" better than men. As little boys grow up, they are not given permission to be emotional the way little girls are. Often, a man needs to cry, but he will not let go and let it happen. He will not express his pain because he believes "real men don't cry." Younger generations are finally learning that this concept of a "real man" is unrealistic, but old habits die hard. In our work with Spatula Ministries, we find that it's the mothers who will open up and shed tears while the fathers try to remain stoic and "unmoved."

But at one time or another, *everybody* cries. The Old Testament tells us that David wept on several occasions.[1] Jesus cried when He learned that His good friend Lazarus had died.[2] With great compassion, Christ also wept over the city of Jerusalem and its inhabitants.[3]

Over the years, researchers have been learning that people who cry frequently enjoy better health overall. It seems that healthy people view tears positively while those who are plagued with various illnesses see tears as unnecessary, even humiliating.

Students in medical school, and even practicing MDs, are urged not to give tranquilizers to weeping patients but to let tears do their own therapeutic work. Laughter and tears are natural medicines. They both allow us to reduce stress and let out our negative feelings so we can recharge. Tears are one of the body's best natural resources.

While modern science didn't fully recognize the value of tears until quite recently, poets have always known intuitively that crying is beneficial. As Shakespeare put it:

TO WEEP IS TO MAKE LESS THE DEPTH OF GRIEF.[4]

Alfred, Lord Tennyson once wrote about a woman who had learned that her husband had been killed. "She must weep," wrote Tennyson, "or she will die."[5]

Old Glory Brings Tears to Bill's Eyes

Most of us shed tears more often than we want to admit. I read somewhere that sadness accounts for 49 percent of weeping; happiness, 21 percent; and the other 30 percent is due to other emotions such as anger, fear, and empathy. Tears reflect our very humanity. The driven and successful executive breaks into tears while reading about homeless people as he rides the subway. The high-powered attorney weeps when he hears a Mozart concerto.

And every Memorial Day, it never fails. When the flags are unfurled and the bands play the patriotic songs, Bill brushes a tear or two from his eyes. I can practically feel the lump of patriotism in his throat.

If you have suffered deep grief and you find you cannot cry, you may need the help of a professional counselor. A nun who read a copy of *Geranium* that had found its way into her convent wrote to tell me she had been a member of a Roman Catholic order for thirty years. Her mother had died tragically in an accident on the very day she was taking her to enter the convent. The nun admits, "It's thirty years later and I'm just beginning to deal with her death."

Her letter goes on to say that she was blamed for her mother's death—if she hadn't planned to enter the convent, the trip would never have been made and the accident would never have happened. "For the last couple of years, I've been seeing someone for help. It's taken thirty years for me to cry," she wrote.

Sometimes we wonder just how much weeping should be controlled. The best answer is that tears should not be controlled as much as they should be ALLOWED. A man rushed his daughter to a local hospital after she had experienced a bad fall. Tears were pouring down the father's cheeks, and the emergency room doctor ordered him to stop crying. Perhaps the father's weeping made the doctor nervous; I'm not sure. But clearly the doctor was wrong. Most people would benefit from crying more often, particularly when they're under heavy stress.

Perhaps the best description of healthy tears comes from Charles Dickens's story, *Oliver Twist*. Mr. Bumble is a less-than-sympathetic character, but he's got the right idea when he declares that crying, "opens the lungs, washes the countenance, exercises the eyes, and softens the temper."

So, cry away. Loretta Young, an actress who was paid to "cry on cue," proved she knew something about real tears when she said:

TEARS WILL MELT THE HEART THAT IS
FROZEN IN GRIEF.

Two Marines Paid Me That Dreaded Call

Readers of the *Love Line*, as well as my other books, know that I divide the grief process into three stages: 1. PANIC AND SHOCK, 2. SUFFERING, and 3. RECOVERY. Another tool that I use to help folks deal with grief is a sheet outlining the steps for dealing with pain: CHURNING, BURNING, YEARNING, LEARNING, and, finally, TURNING.

I've been through these steps several times. Frozen in my memory is a picture of that hot July day when a military staff car stopped in front of our home. It was around 2:00 P.M. Bill was at work, and I was home alone. The scene that unfolded is supposedly what only happens to other people or in movies. Two young men in full-dress marine uniforms knocked at my door. The moment I saw them, I knew what they had come to tell me. Our son, who had been in terrible danger for the past several months, was in peril no longer.

Calmly and gently, a lieutenant explained that Steven's entire unit had been wiped out in a battle near Da Nang. Steve's body would be shipped home in ten days. A telegram was on its way with more information. I don't remember much of what else was said. I wept softly as I heard snatches of information that sounded so unreal. SURELY they were talking about someone else. SURELY they had found the WRONG BOY lying facedown in that rice paddy.

When the neighbors saw the marine staff car at our house, they knew what had happened. Word spread like proverbial wildfire and there was a steady flow of friends coming to our door. At that time, we were the only family in town who had lost a son in the Vietnam conflict. I tried to hold myself together, but the tears just kept coming. I'm afraid I wasn't much of a hostess on that totally UNREAL day.

"This Can't Be Steven . . . It CAN'T!"

In a way, the initial shock of bad news is a cushion that helps you absorb what has happened. For a while, you don't really believe your loved one has died. You deny it, insisting it was someone else who died. Yes, they were shipping some boy's body back, but I told myself that when it arrived, the truth would be known—it would be somebody else and they would somehow find Steven alive.

Just as the two marines had said, in ten days the call came informing us that Steven's body had arrived. Bill was at work, so I drove alone to the mortuary and was ushered into a room containing a hermetically sealed box. I could see through the glass top, but what I saw was surely not Steve. How could this brown, bloated figure in a marine uniform be our son? He looked like someone from another race.

The mortician read to me from an official paper that had arrived with the body, explaining that Steve had lain face-down in a rice paddy for three days before he was found and that accounted for the discoloration and bloating of his face. But I couldn't accept it. I kept insisting, "This can't be Steven. It CAN'T be!"

Patiently, the mortician kept trying to explain what had happened. Finally, there was nothing to do but go home, where we began to plan a memorial service for Steven. We decided to give the service a theme: "Safe in the Arms of Jesus." Bill printed up a brochure with a picture of Steve on the front, one of his last letters on the inside, and the plan of salvation on the back.

It was during that memorial service that I moved from shock and denial into the next stage of grief—suffering. At the graveside, a marine bugler played "Taps," and other marines in full-dress uniform folded the American flag that had been draped on Steven's casket and presented it to us.

A former lieutenant commander and ace fighter pilot in the navy, Bill was grief-stricken but he refused to weep during the memorial service. He had done that earlier at home, sitting in the rocking chair, pounding on the armrest and muttering, "HOW could it happen? He was so YOUNG . . ." For me, the tears were a continuing catharsis that helped wash away my denial. My tears helped me face the fact that Steven was gone. But while I grieved, I could still feel secure because I knew he was safe in the arms of Jesus. He was our "deposit in heaven," and I was comforted by thoughts like this:

DEATH IS NOT EXTINGUISHING THE LIGHT.
IT IS PUTTING OUT THE LAMP
BECAUSE THE DAWN HAS COME.

Five Years Later It Would Happen Again

How could I even imagine then that five years from that *very day*, Bill and I would be at that same cemetery, accepting another flag, presented to us in memory of another son?

Like Steven, Tim died violently, not in a war, but because of a drunken driver on a lonely highway in the Yukon. As hard as Steven's death had been, it had also been something of a relief. We had lived for months in heavy expectancy, scanning the newspaper each morning to be sure his name was not among those reported missing or killed. Tim's death, however, was entirely different.

In the afternoon of August 1, 1973, Tim had called me (collect, of course) from Whitehorse, in the Yukon Territory of northwestern Canada, while on the way home after spending the summer with his friend, Ron, in Alaska. To my surprise, he began telling me about the wonderful things God had been doing in his life. I could hardly believe my ears because, while Tim had always gone along with his Christian upbringing, there had been no light, no fire, no excitement. Now he was on the phone telling me he had a spring in his step and a sparkle in his eye, and he'd be home in five days to tell me what had happened that summer in a church he had attended in Anchorage.

That night at dinner, while I was telling the rest of the family about Tim's call, the phone rang. It was the Royal Canadian Mounted Police with the news that Tim and Ron had been killed instantly when a three-ton truck, driven by a drunk teenager, crossed the center line just outside of Whitehorse and crumpled Tim's little Volkswagen like papier-mâché.

I went through the identical emotions that I had experienced when Steven died. I was plunged again into shock and denial. At first I churned with what felt like a knife in my chest. Later I burned with anger, railing at God for allowing the unthinkable to happen. ANOTHER son taken . . . ANOTHER deposit in heaven . . . wasn't ONE enough?

Again, tears were a blessed relief for me. I didn't deny Tim's death as much as I had Steven's, but I did burn more vehemently because Tim had died so needlessly, so pointlessly, so carelessly.

We buried Tim on August 12, 1973, five years to the day after Steven. Again, we accepted an American flag, this time compliments of the United States Air Force and the Veterans

Administration. (Tim had served briefly in the United States Air Force before being honorably discharged with a medical problem not detected when he took his physical.)

Among the speakers at the memorial service, which was attended by several hundred people, was one of the pastors from the Anchorage church Tim and Ron had attended that summer. He told about the dynamic change in the boys' lives and how they had given public testimony of that change at a baptism where he officiated. As I listened, I thought, *How I wish I could have been there to hear Tim share his faith and then see him be baptized.*

North—to Whitehorse and Anchorage

Two months later, around the middle of October, Bill and I journeyed to Whitehorse to pick up some of Tim's personal belongings that had been salvaged from his car. We also went to the very spot on the highway where he and Ron had been ushered into God's presence. Then we flew to Anchorage to visit the church they had been attending all summer.

Everyone treated us graciously, and a woman on the church staff gave us a tour of the building that included a tape library with THOUSANDS of tapes stored on the shelves. She explained that the church makes a tape of every service, and when there's not much to do during long Alaskan winters, folks use the tapes for entertainment. Some folks can't get to church regularly, but when they do come in from the hinterlands, they often take several tapes back home with them. Not only does the church make tapes of all the services, but many folks bring their own recorders to tape the music or the preaching. In Alaska they like to say that folks aren't bookworms; they're TAPEWORMS!

After seeing all these tapes, I asked what any mother would ask: "Do you have the tape of the night Tim was baptized and gave his testimony?" Sadly, she said she was sorry but the service that night had not been taped.

"Why not?" I questioned. "How come you didn't tape *that* service when everything else is taped?"

She explained that the man who operated the tape-recording equipment had been baptized that night, and no one else had known how to push the buttons!

Coming home from Alaska I felt dejected—that God had surely negated me. Of the thousands of tapes this church had recorded, they had missed the night Tim had given his testimony. How unfair and cruel could God be?

We returned to California and I didn't go back to the cemetery throughout that fall. In early December my mother, who was physically unable to come out for Tim's memorial service, flew out for the Christmas holidays. She wanted to visit Tim's grave, so we drove up to the cemetery even though it was a dreary day, with light rain falling.

As we walked up to the grave, I drew in my breath sharply as I saw freshly turned earth around Tim's gravestone. It had obviously been put in place just a few hours before. I don't know why it had taken so long, from the time of his death until NOW, to get that marker installed. There were pearl-gray clouds in the sky, a light rain falling on his gravestone, and now here was freshly turned dirt!

At that moment, I remembered how, several years before, I had come to this very cemetery with Tim to teach him how to drive. The cemetery was a perfect place because it had wide lanes and good places to practice turns. I taught Tim myself because those were the years when Bill was still recovering from terrible injuries suffered in an accident.

Those were fun times as Tim anticipated getting his driver's license. I recalled going out to get some tacos and coming back to the cemetery where we sat on the grass and ate them. Then we went back to the driving lessons.

Little did I know THEN that I would be coming back to this SAME cemetery, not to practice driving among the headstones but to stand at two of them—Tim's and Steven's.

Suddenly, the events of August flooded back over me—the shock, the pain, the overwhelming feeling of choking or smothering. My mother and I stood there and cried together, trying to find comfort in the cold, drizzling rain.

A Surprise from Nome

Two days later, on December 14, my birthday, a small package came in the mail. It had no return address, but the postmark said NOME, ALASKA. I opened the package and found no letter or note, only a well-worn tape cassette that looked as if it had been used a hundred times. Curious, I put the unlabeled cassette into a tape recorder, and in a few seconds I heard Tim's excited voice!

> My name is Tim Johnson, and I'm third in the group that came up from California. Funny, we were headed for South America. I don't know how we got here but . . . uh . . . the Lord works in miraculous ways. Praise the Lord! I'm glad He did.
>
> I was brought up in a Christian home and Christian schools, but after graduation I departed and went my own way. It wasn't until last December that a friend sat down with me and showed me the real way to the Lord— *the true way.* I was on fire for a couple of months, and then I just fell by the wayside.
>
> It wasn't until I came to Alaska that things really started happening in my life. Since then, I have a smile on my face, and everyone looks at me like I must have been a sour lemon before. But now it's just different, and I'm thankful that I'm here today. Thanks be to God.

The next sounds I heard were splashes as Tim was plunged beneath the waters of baptism. As he came up out of the water, I could hear his triumphant words, "PRAISE THE LORD!"

I sat there, stunned. This was the kid who would get embarrassed if we took him to Knott's Berry Farm for his birthday and sang to him. This was the kid whose idea of fun was bringing home funeral bows from the mortuary where he worked and tying them on our pets. This was the kid we had to bribe with a new set of tires to get him to go to Bible conferences.

This was definitely a MIRACLE!

How the tape found its way into our home was a miracle, too, and it proves God does work in wonderful ways through

His people. Later I learned from the church in Anchorage that one of their members, a bush pilot, had heard about my request for a tape of Tim's baptism service. I'm not sure what bush pilots do (I guess they fly around the bushes a lot) but as this pilot made his many trips into the back country, he began asking folks if anyone had taped the service the night the boys were baptized.

Finally, he found a fisherman from Nome who had visited the church that night and had taped the service. Now I know Nome isn't the end of the world, but I am sure you can see it from there! The bush pilot asked the fisherman to send the tape to me at my home, which he did. It was the best birthday present I could have asked for. It was, indeed, my MIRACLE TAPE.

That tape was played many times during that Christmas season. The tears would roll down my face, but they were tears of joy. In some strange way, listening to Tim's voice helped me accept what had happened. I saw again that God specializes in bringing triumph out of tragedy and joy out of pain. Problems won't disappear because you pretend they don't exist. Your utter helplessness will not magically vanish. Accepting what happens is a vital step to grabbing that rope in the dark that becomes your lifeline. And you want to hang on tightly to that rope because you will probably have more than one encounter with an insidious enemy that attacks anyone going through the grief process: DEPRESSION.

Larry Caused a Different and Deeper Grief

There are many degrees of depression, from mild sorrow to severe, clinical depression that needs professional help. When Steve and Tim died, I went through the grief process with relatively normal amounts of depression. I'd have my bad days, but I never plunged into any prolonged period of feeling hopeless or totally exhausted, as if I just couldn't go on any longer (all typical signs of severe depression).

But two years after Tim died, that fateful Saturday arrived when I learned that Larry, our outstanding, sure-to-succeed (and in some ways most spiritually perceptive) son, was gay. Instead of overwhelming grief, my initial reaction was more like rage. I railed at Larry, screaming, "I'd rather have a son be DEAD than a homosexual!"

We fought, exchanging physical blows and shouting caustic words at each another. The next day Larry left and he was gone for a year without even contacting us. I went into a deep depression that lasted for months. This was something I had not experienced with the deaths of Steve or Tim. With death, there at least is closure. You grieve, you go through the shock, the denial, and the suffering, then at last you come to a recovery time when you begin to get on with your life. But here my son was, in a lifestyle I had been taught was despicable in the eyes of the Lord, and recovery was slow in coming.

My year of suffering is described in other books,[6] but the advice I want to share here is to avoid a common mistake while struggling through the tunnel of depression: DON'T GO INTO ISOLATION. Soon after Larry left home, I began seeing Dr. Wells, a Christian counselor who gave me much practical advice. The trouble was, I refused to accept what he was telling me.

What I wanted Dr. Wells to tell me was that Larry could be FIXED immediately, that all we had to do was claim the promises of Scripture and everything would be okay. But his long experience in counseling homosexuals had proved it wasn't that simple. If Larry were to make any change in his behavior pattern, it would be his decision, not mine.

Dr. Wells kept giving me answers I didn't want to hear to questions I didn't want to ask. Snatches of Bible verses kept running through my mind. Larry was a Christian and anyone in Christ was a NEW CREATION. Christians didn't have to conform to the world; they could be TRANSFORMED by the renewing of their minds so they would be able to do God's perfect will!

And so I became a paradox. I would go out to see Dr. Wells, but I had almost no contact with anyone else, even my own family. Physically, emotionally, and spiritually I became a recluse, spending most of my time in a back bedroom, where I counted roses on the wallpaper, wallowing in self-pity. The pressure inside built to the point where I went all the way to the brink of suicide, looked over the edge, and realized that killing myself was not the answer.[7]

Later, when Spatula Ministries was born, I was able to work with other parents who were buried in deep depression. I learned a secret I wish I had known during that year of isolation, when depression kept me in a black pit of despair where I could not feel God's comfort and love.

Now I know that what I needed was the SUPPORT of other folks who knew what I was going through. Grief work should be done in an atmosphere of healthy dependency. Instead of being isolated, you need to be nurtured, healthily dependent on others for help. Don't be afraid to let others help you. When you are grieving, you cannot think. Let someone else help you with your decisions. Grief work is what friends are for. Remember:

WHEN YOU'RE IN A JAM, GOOD FRIENDS WILL
BRING YOU BREAD WITH PEANUT BUTTER ON IT.

The mail brought a letter from one mom whose son is fifteen and "knows everything." He left home, stayed away a few months, came back, and then left again. Now he chooses to ignore his family, who continues to pray for him daily, not knowing where he is. The mother wrote:

> I didn't realize how long it's been since I smiled. . . . Thank you for your support. I read *Stick a Geranium in Your Hat*, and it kept me from going over the edge. Then, when I wrote to you, you wrote me back. That just blew my mind. . . . Knowing someone else really cares means a lot. I have run into quite a few church people who have never read the list of what NOT to say when a friend is hurting. It would help if others just kept some statements to themselves. If one more person tells me, "Pray, God can do anything," I will scream.

Letters like this one leave me with mixed emotions. I'm glad to hear that a book like *Geranium* can reach out and help parents who are hurting. At the same time, however, the printed page can only do so much. When you're hurting, down the road somewhere you *need someone with skin on*—another person with whom you can talk, share, cry, and maybe even laugh a little. You need people who will bring you the psychological equivalent of bread and peanut butter because they know what kind of jam you are in and they want to help you OUT.

I treasure a letter sent to me by a mom who grieved alone for a long time over the loss of her son, with no help from her husband, who stayed in his own closet of pain. She wrote:

> When you told me to reach out and help someone else in need, I did that—and IT WORKED! We cannot survive by ourselves; we dilute our pain by sharing with others. Trying to get through this by myself didn't work. I thank you for encouraging me to hook up with a network of others and to pour out my energy and love on someone else. All this has helped bring ME through something I thought would never pass. We DO need each other to find the answers though.

Indeed, we do. Whatever your problem, find a support group.[8] These days they are available for alcoholics, drug abusers, workaholics, people with eating disorders, just about any problem imaginable. Originally, Spatula support groups focused specifically on Christian parents whose children are homosexual. Today we also include parents whose children have died, gotten into trouble with the law, or who face other difficulties. Our goal at Spatula is the same as any other support effort: to provide a comfortable setting for hurting folks to come together to bring healing to their wounds.

When we treat a physical wound, it has to be cleaned with antiseptic. Then it may need some stitching up and a sterile bandage to keep it clean. Then it takes time for the wound to heal. Emotional wounds are treated in somewhat the same way. To cleanse our hurts, we have to examine ourselves to evaluate the nature of the pain we feel. We must talk about our feelings and ventilate . . . Ventilate . . . VENTILATE. One of our mottos at Spatula is:

OPENNESS IS TO WHOLENESS
AS SECRETS ARE TO SICKNESS.

The tears I shed over Steven, Tim, and Larry all combined to help me accept the truth that God often allows our hearts to be broken so He can beautify our lives. Floods of adversity may sweep over us, but only so that the light of His presence may shine upon us. As Charles Fox wrote:

DARK WATERS BLOSSOM WHITE IN BREAKING,
HIGH SOULS ARE MADE IN THE UNMAKING.

Fox meant that only when the ocean waves are broken into spray will oxygen cause the waves to reflect the glory of the sunlight. Are you in the midst of a great storm of grief? Are your cherished dreams all shattered? Remember, God has a purpose in allowing this. He chooses to fashion us from brokenness into a life that will reflect His glory. We are like stained-glass windows. By ourselves we have no light, but when the "SON" shines through, we sparkle and glow. When darkness sets in, our true beauty is revealed only if there is true light from within. And remember:

IF THERE WERE NO GRIEF TO HOLLOW OUR HEARTS
THERE WOULD BE NO ROOM FOR JOY!

Bugaboo Busters

EXPERIENCE IS WHAT YOU GET
WHEN YOU'RE LOOKING FOR SOMETHING ELSE.

It's not so much what happens to you;
it's how you handle the happenings.

IF IT DOESN'T KILL YOU,
IT WILL MAKE YOU STRONGER.

Things NOT To Do When You're Feeling Blue:
Don't weigh yourself.
Don't watch *Old Yeller.*
Don't go near a chocolate shop.
Don't open your credit-card bill.
Don't go shopping for a new bathing suit.

WHICH DO I NEED MORE?
TO PULL MYSELF TOGETHER,
OR LET MYSELF GO?

Ashleigh Brilliant, Pot-shot
#4600 © 1988.

There are many tears in the heart
that never reach the eye.

SUDDEN DEATH IS SUDDEN GLORY . . .

Engraved on the headstone of a beloved son:
"HE'S NOT GONE . . . HE'S JUST GONE ON AHEAD."

I know things are tough right now, but just remember . . . every flower that ever bloomed had to go through a whole lot of dirt to get there!

WHEN LIFE BRINGS TOO MUCH PRESSURE,
TEARS ARE THE SAFETY VALVES OF THE HEART.

If the meaning of my life doesn't soon become clear,
I may have to request an extension.
Ashleigh Brilliant, Pot-shot
#4705 © 1988.

From the Spatula mailbag:
I'm forever indebted to you for your books,
for the laughter (I haven't lost my sense of
humor—my situation is too hysterical for
anything except to laugh at), and for your
prayers. Please call my name sometime
when you're traveling through my part of
the country on your Exercycle in your Joy
Room.[9]

HE WASHES OUR EYES WITH TEARS THAT WE MIGHT SEE.[10]

You have seen me tossing and turning through the
night. You have collected all my tears and preserved
them in YOUR bottle! You have recorded every one
in your book. (Ps. 56:8 TLB, emphasis mine).

4

Yesterday Is Experience . . .
Tomorrow Is Hope . . .
Today Is Getting from One to the Other

*M*any of us are familiar with Erma Bombeck's line: "Guilt is the gift that keeps on giving." As I've done my own grief work and helped others with theirs, I've learned there is another "companion gift" that comes right along with guilt: It's called REGRET, and it keeps on giving, too, if you let it.

In fact, it's hard to say if regret leads to guilt or if it's the other way around. It's one of those chicken/egg questions that doesn't matter. When tragedy strikes, dealing with both guilt *and* regret is almost always part of your grief work.

Perhaps in all the world there is nobody more susceptible to feeling guilty than a mother. Often I talk with mothers who have lost children in death or into a lifestyle that is sinful or dangerous. In many cases, they have been robbed of their joy by guilt feelings. *If only* they had done this or that . . . *if only* they had been a better parent, then their child would have turned out right.

As one mother of a wayward son put it, "I have tried many times to 'Give it all to the Lord,' and I thought I had, but I guess I keep doing what you did and keep picking up the burden again myself. I am harboring a lot of guilt over this and asking myself, 'What did I do wrong?'"

Like so many mothers who are Christians, this mom knows the central teaching of Christianity: Our sins are covered by the blood of Jesus. As far as He is concerned, no matter WHAT we have done, He cannot see it anymore. We are cleansed and forgiven. If we truly believe our sins are forgiven, we can get on with life and experience the joy of God's forgiveness.

Why, then, are so many of us still crippled with guilt feelings? If our guilt is real, perhaps we have never really dealt with it. We must be honest with God about what we have done wrong. We must confess our failures and accept our weaknesses—admitting that we are not perfect. (This is harder for some folks than you might think.)

Once we admit our failures, we must relinquish ALL of them to God. Then we reach out and accept His cleansing forgiveness. The Bible so clearly says what many of us know from childhood: "If we confess our sins, he is faithful and just to forgive us our sins, and to cleanse us from all unrighteousness" (1 John 1:9 KJV). In this familiar verse is God's golden guarantee of cleansing and forgiveness, but so many folks don't seem to really believe it. They believe their sin is too great or their failures too severe. They tell me, "I'm just not worthy of God's forgiveness."

My answer to that is that none of us is worthy, but all of us are eligible. This little verse by my friend, Ruth Harms Calkin, says it well:

"Dear God: I have sinned against heaven and against you.
I am no longer worthy to be called your child."

"My child, I know, I know . . .
but my Son is forever worthy to be called your Savior."[1]

Her words remind me of one of my favorite riddles:

WHAT CAN BE WHITER THAN SNOW AND DEEPER
THAN THE SEA?
Answer:

MY SINS, WHICH CHRIST MAKES WHITER THAN
SNOW THROUGH HIS LOVE WHICH IS FAR DEEPER
THAN THE SEA.

Guilt Feelings Breed More Guilt Feelings

Some folks can read all this and then say, "Barbara, I know
you're right. I've heard all this since I was a child. But I still feel
guilty, and that makes me feel even MORE guilty!"

If you can't shake guilt feelings, you can try separating true
guilt from false. Lots of folks are carrying burdens of false guilt,
thinking they have failed when they really have not. Again,
moms suffer most from guilt feelings. They want to take on re-
sponsibility for everything their kids have done, and when they
go wrong through their own choices, Mom still thinks, "It
surely must have been MY fault."

So, how do we separate true guilt from false?" Sometimes
it's simple; other times it's difficult, but you might want to try
this solution: Why not give ALL your guilt to Jesus, the true *and*
the false? Let Him separate it out and make the final judgments.
Let Him decide what is true about the gray areas of your life,
where the answers aren't in simple black and white.

You see, the good news is that Jesus was nailed to a cross so
you could stop nailing yourself to a cross—of true *or* false
guilt. Accept His forgiveness and you can live a guilt-free life
from here on out! The following letter is a perfect example of
a mom who wants to trust God but just can't seem to shake her
heavy load of guilt:

> I have *so much* guilt from my past adult life (I'm fifty-two
> now), that sometimes I can hardly carry my load. But
> when I read the *Love Line* or a certain passage in the Bible,
> I'm gently reminded that I don't have to carry that load
> anymore. I feel good for a while, but before I know it, I've
> strapped all that guilt to my back again.
>
> Oh, Barb, it's so heavy! Sometimes—no, a lot of the
> time—I'm scared to death my precious daughter will follow

in my footsteps. In some ways she already has. But let me stop whining and give glory and praise. God worked a miracle in her life and she finally finished a technical training program (at the age of 30!).

Sometimes I wonder why I had a child. I've never been a good mother. When she was little I was a drug addict, and I live in constant fear that she might take that path. Anything good that she is today is because my wonderful mother raised her during those years.

I know Jesus died for my sins, but it's just too hard to accept it. I am a drug-free Christian today and very thankful for it. But I am not a guilt-free Christian.

What this dear mom means is that she doesn't *feel* guilt free. If she's truly trusting in Christ, her sins of the drug years are wiped away. What she still feels are those nagging doubts that come from false guilt, and she probably has many regrets, as well. We know that guilt and regret go hand in hand. They are sisters who have taught me a valuable lesson:

WHEN YOU BROOD OVER YOUR TROUBLES,
YOU WILL ONLY HATCH DESPAIR.

I Know What It Is to Feel Regret

As I look back on the tragedies that caused so much grief in our family, I remember my frequent wrestling matches with pangs of regret. When Bill suffered a crippling accident on an isolated mountain road, I regretted that I hadn't gone with him instead of coming up later with the boys in our other car. We had volunteered to be counselors for our church youth group that weekend, and I had made a trip up the mountain earlier that day to help get the retreat center ready. On the way down, I had noticed that construction crews had been doing some repair work on the road and that there was some debris lying about. I assumed the workers would clear it away before leaving for the night, and I never thought of it again—until after I found Bill lying in a pool of blood and broken glass several hours later.

Somehow, Bill recovered—no, not "somehow," God healed him after the doctors said he would be blind and like a vegetable for the rest of his life, which they said wouldn't be more than five years. But just two years later I felt the bitter pangs of regret again after agreeing to sign the necessary papers to allow Steven to enter the Marine Corps early, before his eighteenth birthday. I rationalized at the time, saying, "He'll go in anyway in a few more months, so why not let him join now with all his buddies? Besides, the war is decelerating and he'll never see any action."

But after Steven joined, the war heated up again and Steven had to go to Vietnam after all. When the news came that he had been killed in action, the demons of regret gnawed at my mind. WHY had I signed that paper? I kept thinking that his death was MY fault because I'd let him join the service early, finish his training, and be shipped to Vietnam, where he wound up on that particular battlefield near Da Nang on July 28, 1968.

Five years later, when Tim was killed by a drunk driver on his way home from Alaska, regret struck me again. In our last phone conversation, I had suggested that he ship his little Volkswagen by boat so he could fly home. It was an extravagant idea—something probably only a mother would think of—and Tim sort of laughed it off because he didn't have a clue about how he could ship a car from the Yukon wilderness.

Later, after we had buried our second deposit in heaven, I remembered that conversation. I had felt uneasy about Tim's driving the little Volkswagen over those thousands of miles on a five-day trip. If only I had insisted that he fly home instead. I went over it again and again in my mind, thinking of how cheap it would have been to have shipped the car home compared with having Tim pay with his life.

Two more years passed and pangs of regret stabbed me again over how I had responded to Larry when I learned that he was gay. My self-righteous rage drove him from our home. I regretted my anger, which eventually turned inward and became depression.

Over the years, I've worked my way through all these regrets, feeling a pang now and then, but the sting has flattened out.

I've learned that regret is the pain we feel when we compare what IS with what MIGHT HAVE BEEN. Regret is one of the most universal feelings because at times we all feel pangs of conscience over what we have done or not done.

We cannot escape having regrets any more than we can escape having pain. For every choice we make, we give up a host of other options, and that often leaves us open to feelings of regret. Why didn't we make the OTHER choice? We don't know, but now wish we had.

Regret's favorite words are "If only" and "What if?" *If only* I had remembered to tell Bill the mountain road was being worked on and to be extra careful. *What if* I hadn't signed for Steven to go into the marines before he was of legal age? *If only* I had somehow talked Tim into shipping his car home and flying back home from Alaska. *What if* I could have been more gentle instead of angry when I learned that Larry was gay?

How would our lives have been different *if only* all my "what if's" had not happened?

Don't Play the Self-Blame Game

But to dwell on "if only" and "what if" is to play the self-blame game. Self-blame over the past leads to depression in the present and poor decisions for the future. Coming to terms effectively with your regrets takes self-compassion, not self-blame.

"Coming to terms" doesn't mean excusing ourselves for failures. It does mean forgiving ourselves by evaluating the past realistically, admitting our limitations, accepting God's forgiveness, and then moving on. It has been said:

WE CRUCIFY OURSELVES BETWEEN TWO THIEVES—
REGRET FOR YESTERDAY AND FEAR OF TOMORROW.

Regret is a key reason why holidays produce stress with many sad memories. A loved one's birthday, a wedding anniversary, and especially Christmas focus our attention on the difference between what was, what might have been, and what is reality for us today.

You cannot change the past, but you can control your own attitude. So what if you made a bad decision? You don't have to wallow in guilt forever. Examining regret can help us understand our values and why we are unhappy over the past. It can build a bridge to a better future. Through the years I've learned a number of ways to HARNESS REGRET and make it a positive tool for wholeness. Here are some of them:

1. Reframe Your Perspective

When feelings of regret creep in, try viewing the situation in a different light. Don't put yourself down with thoughts like, "I wasn't good enough or smart enough or wise enough . . ." Give yourself the benefit of the doubt and say, "What I had to offer wasn't appreciated . . . I did my best . . . I'll try to do better next time." As somebody said:

IT'S NO DISGRACE TO FAIL,
BUT IT'S A SIN TO DO LESS THAN YOUR BEST.

It's funny how your mind plays tricks on you when you're struggling with grief. It took me a long time to see that allowing Steven to enter the marines early is not what killed him. In a war, you can get killed at any time, any place. It all happens in God's economy, not ours.

And the same was true of Tim. I regretted not INSISTING that he ship his little Volkswagen home from the Yukon and fly instead, but obviously, Tim might have done this and the plane could have crashed! We cannot control these things, and when we are tempted to second-guess the Lord, it's good to poke a little fun at ourselves by imagining that we have just received a little memo from Him saying:

RELAX! YOU ARE NOT RESPONSIBLE FOR EVERYTHING
IN THE UNIVERSE. THAT'S STILL *MY* JOB.

Love,
God

One of the best ways to reframe your perspective is to fine-tune your sense of humor. The past becomes easier to bear when you view it through the prism of humor. When I was going through the tragedies that hit our family, I never would have believed I'd be sharing these painful parts of my life in a humorous way, bringing laughter as well as insight to others. When we are able to laugh at ourselves, it reminds us that no one is perfect, and it makes an imperfect, even cruel, world easier to bear.

2. Surrender the Need to Always Be Right

Somebody said you have to choose:

DO YOU WANT TO BE RIGHT—OR HAPPY?

I'm not talking about compromising your integrity; I'm talking about not always having your own way, allowing others to make their choices—as bad as those choices may be.

When Larry left, my regret over being so angry with him sent me into deep depression. Things were spinning out of my control, and I felt helpless. Eventually I understood that surrendering control doesn't mean compromising; in fact, not needing to be in control— being willing to say, "Whatever, Lord!"—is a source of tremendous strength.

But as you surrender the need to always be right you see the importance of repairing relationships that have been strained, or even broken. Even if it bruises your ego, mending fences is one of the most practical ways to deal with regret and guilt. Together, Larry and I discovered:

THE BEST EXERCISE FOR GOOD RELATIONSHIPS
IS BENDING OVER BACKWARD.

As one mother of a homosexual son put it: "The big thing I'm learning through all this 'gay stuff' is that LOVE must never stop. It's our biggest asset and does more good than anything else!" She is so right, and her words remind me of a little prayer:

LORD, WHEN I AM WRONG, MAKE ME WILLING
TO CHANGE;
WHEN I AM RIGHT, MAKE ME EASY TO LIVE WITH.

3. Seize Opportunities to Refresh Others

Doing something positive toward another person is a practical approach to feeling good about yourself. Cynics may say that all you're doing is "watering down your guilt," but the Scriptures are right: As you refresh others, you yourself are refreshed.[2]

So live in the present and make the most of your opportunities to enjoy your family and friends. Don't use excuses such as, "I don't have the time right now . . . I'll save that for later . . . I'm too tired . . ."

Regret has a way of trapping you in a rut that can become a deep hole of despair. One way to get out of the rut of regret is to do things that matter to you. When Steven died in Vietnam, Bill and I started a ministry to reach out to other parents who had lost sons in the war. Then, when Tim died in that head-on crash, we expanded our ministry to help others who had suffered similar tragedies.

Later, after I discovered Larry's homosexuality and he vanished without a trace, I started Spatula Ministries to help parents who needed "scraping off the ceiling" because they, too, had learned their children were struggling with homosexual feelings. Perhaps you aren't ready for something as ambitious as starting a ministry, but you can still reach out in your own way.

One woman who has had years of illness in her family (including her own recent hysterectomy) wrote, "I can't do what you do; however, I hurt so for people and I do enjoy sending hundreds of notes, cards, and little books to try to encourage and uplift them."

Exactly! There are lots of positive steps you can take *away* from the path of regret and *onto* the path of hope.

It's true that what the world needs now is love, but I believe it needs hope even more. One of my favorite sayings is this:

HOPE IS OXYGEN FOR YOUR SOUL

I love the following letter from a mom who understands what it means to be plunged into hopelessness and then find hope after all:

> Oh, Barbara, I'll put it briefly. My son is on drugs—has been for years. My oldest daughter is pregnant—again—and still not married. My husband left me for another woman two years ago. The resulting divorce sent my youngest daughter into her second nervous breakdown. Then my pregnant older daughter caught *her* boyfriend with another woman.
>
> Guess what? We're Christians! Raised all my kids as Christians. Lived the life in front of them as best I could. *Now* God has given me *HOPE* again. I'm not sure it was any one thing, just a slow process of getting to know God better and going on (as you say in your books) *one day at a time.*

What to Do When You're Fresh Out of Hope

This mom's letter makes my heart smile because it reminds me that hope is like the biblical manna the Israelites ate in the wilderness. You need to gather a new supply each day, and sometimes you get so involved in battling your own "wilderness" that you forget to do so.

I recall speaking at a weekend conference and then catching a plane for home. We came in over Los Angeles at night, and from my window seat I saw thousands of flickering lights below. The pilot's voice crackled over the intercom informing us he was making his final approach, but I really didn't hear much of what he was saying. I was thinking about ALL those lights, realizing that each one represented a home where there was (or probably would be) pain of some kind, because pain *is* inevitable in this life.

My imagination started working overtime, and I began seeing each light as a painful abscess that needed to be drained—but how? I have always loved the bit of wisdom that says:

> EVEN IF IT BURNS A BIT LOW AT TIMES,
> THE SECRET OF LIFE IS TO ALWAYS
> KEEP THE FLAME OF HOPE ALIVE.

Gazing below, I began to fear my "flame" had flickered out someplace along the way because it all seemed so overwhelmingly HOPELESS. Then it struck me that I knew better. Hope was supposed to be my specialty, and here I was seemingly drained of all hope myself! I realized that speaking at all those conferences had sapped my spirit. I was suffering a mild case of burnout. My batteries needed recharging, and what better place to go for that than the promises of Scripture?

> I WILL . . . TRANSFORM HER VALLEY
> OF TROUBLES INTO A DOOR OF HOPE.
> (Hos. 2:15 TLB)

> THERE IS HOPE FOR YOUR FUTURE,
> SAYS THE LORD, AND YOUR CHILDREN
> WILL COME AGAIN TO THEIR OWN
> LAND. (Jer. 31:17 TLB)

In the next few moments my vision from the airliner window cleared. The scene below DID NOT represent hopeless pain. Instead, each flickering light in that giant sprawl known as the L.A. Basin was really a place where God's redeeming love could bring hope if only those in pain were willing to LET HIM IN. Then the abscesses could be lanced, and healing could begin.

Perhaps another reason that sea of light looked so hopeless at first glance was because I often feel overwhelmed by the mail and telephone calls I receive—literally thousands each year. I'm only ONE person and cannot begin to meet all the needs of these folks who contact me. But it helps when I realize that they are receiving help by just verbalizing their frustration, ventilating their anger, and most importantly, draining their pain.

Sometimes folks call me and go on and on . . . and ON. I usually say very little as I listen to them, but as they hang up, they often say, "Oh, you have helped me SO MUCH!" I am amazed, knowing that I only listened and prayed with them. In many cases that was all that was needed. It has been said:

TALKING IS SHARING—LISTENING IS CARING.

When the "Right Answers" Don't Seem to Work

We've all heard that when we get to the end of our rope, we're supposed to tie a knot, get a good grip, and swing! Do you know what that knot at the end of your rope is? Of course you do:

HANG ON TO THE *HOPE!*

Christians have the assurance that as long as Jesus is with them, they are more than conquerors. Jesus is our hope. He is God's gift of grace to us. Whenever we say that something is hopeless, we are slamming the door in the face of God.

While that is true, sometimes the circumstances of life leave us so devastated that hope is buried in a black pit of hopelessness. The first time our son, Larry, left home to enter the gay lifestyle and refused to contact us for many months, my fires of hope burned so low that one day I thought they had gone out.

I drove up a viaduct near Disneyland, fully intending to drive over the edge and take my own life. Just as I reached the top, however, I began wondering if the fall to another freeway below would do the whole job. Perhaps I'd just be maimed and wind up making baskets in the home for the bewildered. I couldn't do it.

All hope was gone—even the hope of putting myself out of my misery. And that's when I told the Lord I just couldn't go on any longer. I just couldn't carry the burden of our son one more day. I gave Larry to Him; I *relinquished* him and sealed

NEVER GIVE UP!

the agreement with two words that have become a motto I live by daily:

WHATEVER, LORD!

In other books I've described the incredible change that came over me almost instantaneously as I whispered those words. Hope and the desire to live returned, and I drove back home where the very next day we had a call from Larry, breaking a year-long silence.

This poem by a dear Spatula friend says it all so well. My thanks to Anna Jean McDaniel for sharing it.

> If I can say, "Whatever, Lord,"
> When my heart is about to break,
> When it's full of despair and overcome
> With an uncontrollable ache.

CHAPTER 4

If I can say, "Whatever, Lord,"
And nail my boy to that tree,
Will the burden be lifted from my soul?
Then will my heart be free?

Free from the fear that chills me so
In the dark and friendless night,
When my tired eyes refuse to close
And I wait for the morning light?

If I can say, "Whatever, Lord,"
Will He reach with His arms of love
And wrap me 'round with the Comforter
Sent from heaven above?

If I can say, "Whatever, Lord,"
Will He hear my anguished cries?
Will He answer quickly and not delay
Before hope within me dies?

Others have found the answer
As they've dared to say the word,
What more can I do but follow,
And whisper, "Whatever . . . Lord"?

Anna Jean McDaniel, 1993

Larry came back into our lives, but on a tentative basis with only a superficial relationship. Two years later he telephoned to tell me he had a lover in his life. He said he never wanted to see any of us again and he planned to change his name and disown us. In the years that followed, Spatula was born and became a refuge for other parents whose hope had waned because they had lost children to the gay lifestyle or to another detour situation.

Several years went by, and we didn't hear from Larry. My flame of hope flickered low at times, especially when Mother's Day approached. Personal experience had taught me that Mother's Day could be full of sadness instead of joy. I wanted to reach out and encourage other moms who were longing to hear from their children, but instead, like me, they were waiting for the calls that never came. They were searching the mail for the

cards or letters that never arrived. But when you have a prodigal kid who is bringing you heartache, you have to remember:

GOD WILL DO WHAT HE PROMISES!

Meanwhile, we have to get on with the business of life and
not get stalled on the tracks and run over by the train of doubts.
Around the first of May that year, I made a trip to a nearby
mall, where I poked around in a gift shop, all the while dread-
ing the upcoming Mother's Day because of all the heaviness I
knew it would bring. I was thinking about HOPE and how to
instill it in myself and other moms who might be sinking with
despair. Suddenly I came upon a darling little rag doll enclosed
in a box that said, "Hello! My name is Hope!" I took the doll out
of the box to look at it and saw a little sign on her blouse that
also said, "I'M HOPE!"
I thought how neat it was of the Lord to let me stumble on to
that bit of encouragement, and I bought the doll on the spot.
Leaving the store with my newly purchased friend tucked
snugly under my arm in a shopping bag, I hurried home with
thoughts of hope filling my mind. Yes, as long as a child is alive,
THERE IS HOPE! Even if it is not happening right now, and our
hearts are sick because our hope is deferred, we cannot give the
final score on a life until the game is over. Always remember:

EVERY SAINT HAS A PAST . . .
EVERY SINNER HAS A FUTURE!

The problem is that many parents try to play Holy Spirit for
their kids. We try to bring conviction to them, and instead we
only bring condemnation. It is the job of the Holy Spirit to con-
vict. That is why many kids become resentful when parents try
to force God on them. We have to give them to God and then
take our hands OFF. In *Splashes of Joy in the Cesspools of Life*, I
explained how I do this, including an illustration of the image
I hold in my heart as I let go. Because so many folks have com-
mented on how meaningful this is, I'm repeating it on page 80.

Giving Your Loved One to God

In your mind, picture yourself putting your loved one into a beautifully wrapped gift box. Next, imagine yourself climbing a long flight of stairs, carrying your precious package to the top, where Jesus sits on the throne of God. Put the package at Jesus' feet and wait until He opens it and takes your loved one in His arms. Be sure Jesus has your loved one in His grip, and believe that He will *never* let go. Now comes the crucial moment. Turn around and walk back down the stairs. Halfway down, pause to see that your loved one is safe in Jesus' arms as He says, "No one will ever take this precious one out of My hands, and I will never let him go." As you continue down the stairs, hear yourself praying, *Lord, that settles it. I have given (name) to You and have taken my hands off. Do Your work in (his or her) life as You see fit.*

As one mom admitted, though, this isn't always as easy as it sounds:

> I want you to know that I carry in my billfold the picture of the mother who is looking back after giving her child to Jesus. It's a reminder of when I gave my son to Him (actually, I have had to do it more than once—I have a tendency to take him back). I still have doubts and fears a lot of the time, but I know He will take good care of him.

Giving your child to Jesus is like addressing a package, wrapping it up and putting on a label, and then being able to send it without any special directions of where it should go. Could I love Larry, pray for him, and let God do with his life what He wanted to do, minus my instructions? Could I be content knowing that Larry was trained in the way he should go and I had to relinquish him completely?

It was a much better Mother's Day because I knew Larry was God's property and God always goes after the prodigal!

All the things I felt back then are expressed so beautifully in this little essay by Ruth L. Clemmons:

When You Lose a Child

"It's the fault of the parents," she said with authority. "Children go wrong because their parents don't bring them up in the nurture and admonition of the Lord."

Looking around the circle, I realized I was not the only mother in the group who had been deeply hurt by one of her children.

This message was not new to me, for I had sat in a congregation several years earlier and heard the speaker intone: "Children will not go wrong if parents teach them right. If you put good seed in the ground, you will get good plants." My feelings of failure had been overwhelming. . . .

Our son was brought up in the church. He had been exposed to Bible reading and prayer in the home from his earliest years and had made a profession of faith at nine years of age. I did not work outside the home. I was always there when he came home. We made cookies together, and his friends were welcome. He and his father had worked together on Cub Scout projects; they had gone fishing, boating, and camping together.

Then came the rebellion. When it became extreme, we sought professional advice. Over a period of several years, we made many trips to counselors, from ministers to mental health experts. We wept many tears, spent many sleepless nights, and agonized through many days. But our son left us and went his own way. We had tried to nurture the young plant, but the outside influences and other factors beyond our control were too strong.

As we looked back in those days, we wondered if the break could have been avoided. Were we too strict? Were we too lenient? Did we hover too closely? Did we praise too little? Did we pray too little? Would a strong church youth program have helped?

What We Have Learned

We do not know. Some things we learned over the years as we struggled with our grief and guilt.

First, we found *such a problem can adversely affect a marital relationship.* The constant talking, soul-searching, and seeking a scapegoat can be dangerous. It took conscious and continuous effort to keep the romance in our marriage.

Second, *time will make a difference.* We know of an estranged son who returned to his parents, and they now have a beautiful relationship with him and his lovely wife. Our son has not solved his personal problems, but we have been reconciled. He phones occasionally from faraway places to say, "Happy birthday" or "Merry Christmas." For this, we are thankful.

Third, we have learned to *accept him where he is,* and to say, "Thank You, Lord, for what You are doing in the life of our son, even though we cannot see it now. We know that You love him, and we leave him in Your hands."

Finally, we have learned *this grief, like bereavement, goes through several stages.* We have experienced the numbness, the pain, the resentment, the depression. We can never dismiss our son from our thoughts, but we have come to accept that each person must ultimately be responsible for his own life. Therefore, we are no longer tormented by regrets. We think we know what kind of life would bring our son fulfillment, but the choice is his. We can only continue to assure him of our love and to pray for his happiness.

We do not grieve as those who have no hope. God has given us peace, and we have a full life. We are finally free.

Several more years went by before we heard from Larry. And then the prodigal DID return, asking forgiveness for all the pain he had caused us and telling us he stood clean before the Lord!

But what if Larry had not returned? Then all that I say above would still hold true. An ancient playwright wrote the familiar line: "Where there's life, there's hope."[3] The other day I read something that reversed that line to say:

WHERE THERE'S HOPE, THERE'S LIFE.

Yes, hope *can* give us life. It can provide energy that otherwise would drain completely away if we tried to operate only in our own strength. Hope is so life-giving that the apostle Paul named it as one of three things that will remain long after prophesies, knowledge, and signs and wonders have passed away: "And now these three remain: faith, hope and love" (1 Cor. 13:13 NIV).

When I read that wonderful verse, it always takes me right back to that night on the airliner when I looked down at all those lights and felt hopelessly overwhelmed. It reminded me that what God *promises* and *does* is our only real basis for hope each day. Fatigue, anxiety, and regret may come, but keep looking for hope, and remember:

IT'S BETTER TO FORGET AND SMILE
THAN TO REMEMBER AND BE UPSET.

Bugaboo Busters

We learn from experience. For example, you never wake up your second baby just to see it smile.

WHEN YOUR HEART HURTS,
YA GOTTA USE YOUR HEAD.

Be ready to suffer anything from anyone, but do not be the cause of another's sorrow.

ABOUT TOMORROW,
LET GOD WORRY!

If you're trying to let go:

1. Expect it to hurt—for a while.

2. Develop other interests. Don't make your children responsible for your happiness.

3. Don't play travel agent and try to send your kids on guilt trips.

4. Remember, a child is a loan from God, not your personal possession.

5. Also remember that parents are supposed to give their kids road maps, but they don't have to pave the road for them.

THE BEST BRIDGE BETWEEN DESPAIR AND HOPE
IS A GOOD NIGHT'S SLEEP.

Hope is the thing with feathers
That perches in the soul,
And sings the tune without the words
And never stops at all.

Emily Dickinson[4]

WHAT WE WEAVE IN TIME
WE MUST WEAR IN ETERNITY.

From the Spatula mailbag:
I was beginning to think I was weird for the way I felt. Shortness of breath, not wanting to be around people, feeling anger and hate, and thinking I must be the worst mother in the world. Thank you for letting

me see your scars. Now I know there is
hope for me also. Even though I am in the
tunnel, I know there will be light again.

Hope is faith
holding out its hand
in the dark.

What happiness for those whose guilt has been
forgiven! What joys when sins are covered over!
What relief for those who have confessed their sins
and God has cleared their record. (Ps. 32:1 TLB)

5

Cast Your Bread upon the Waters, and It Will Come Back Pretzels

*I*n the mail recently came a card from a faithful Spatula supporter who knows the heavy burdens of this ministry. One line from his card sticks in my mind:

Sometimes, I wonder how (and why) you stick with all your work!

In the same mail that day, God sent me refreshment from another friend who wrote, "Roll back the pages of memory now and then, Lord, and show me where You've brought me from, and where I could have been. But remember I am human, and humans forget. So remind me, remind me, dear Lord!"

She also quoted a well-known definition of evangelism that she had read in one of Chuck Colson's books: "Evangelism is one beggar telling another beggar where he found bread." And then her letter continued, "That is what Spatula does that helps so much. You share where you found water, and in time, others of us find that the well still works. Then the water running down our lips encourages others to get their drink."

When I make a fool of myself...
   you are the one who doesn't laugh
When everyone but me is invited
   you are the one who refuses to go without me
When I don't get the joke
   you are the one who explains it to me
When I consider all the people
   I've ever known and
all the friends I've ever had...
   you are the one!

Phil. 1:3-6

© "Sonshine Promises" created by Gretchen Clasby, Cedar Hill Studio.
Used by permission.

Her words stayed in my mind for the rest of the day. In a few sentences, she had caught the spirit of what Spatula is all about—bringing encouragement to folks who are feeling hopeless, alone, and so desperately in need of someone to reach out to let them know there is a friend who understands and cares. We often say:

A FRIEND WILL STRENGTHEN YOU WITH HER PRAYERS,
BLESS YOU WITH HER LOVE,
AND ENCOURAGE YOU WITH HER HOPE.

In this chapter, we will focus on some principles for being a FRIEND and an ENCOURAGER. From firsthand experience I can say we really can't have too many encouragers in this worry world.

When I discovered Larry was gay, I panicked, and my rage drove him from our home. Then I became so depressed I went into isolation, refusing to talk to friends or family for almost a year. That was a big mistake because I didn't understand the power in the group-oriented approach to healing. In fact, I didn't even KNOW there was such an approach—where hurting parents find other hurting parents and they help each other, no matter where they are on the pain continuum. Some have experienced healing themselves, and they can share what they've learned. Others still have raw, bleeding edges and need all the bandages they can get.

Since Spatula Ministries focuses on parents of homosexuals who have "hit the ceiling" over their children, we often hear from folks who feel isolated or who want to be. In other words, they want to withdraw because they feel like such utter failures. One mom wrote to say:

> My son has been in the gay lifestyle and with the same partner for many years. We have a good relationship and I really care for his friend, but I still have trouble occasionally dealing with the embarrassment their lifestyle brings me. I love them and can accept them, but I still struggle at times. I pray and give it all to God, but I still find I just can't talk to others about my son. Is this normal?

Yes, those feelings are very normal. We shouldn't forget:

FEELINGS ARE THE BREATH OF THE HUMAN HEART.

I heard from another mom who put it this way: "I'm an 'in-the-closet' mother of a homosexual son. There haven't been many times I've been able to even say that much. But healing is coming, and your newsletter is a help."

What's It Like in the Closet?

There is a cynical saying going around these days:

WHEN THE KIDS COME OUT OF THE CLOSET
THE PARENTS GO IN.

Parents often come to our Spatula meetings and say their child has just informed them of who he is and that HE feels relieved. Now that his family knows, he says, he's free to "be himself." The parents, of course, are in a state of shock. Ironically, a child feels released when he comes out, but all it does for the parents is put them into their own private prison of isolation.

I know there are THOUSANDS of parents out there who have swept their problems under the rug and then crawled under it themselves to live in dark secrecy. I know how they feel. When you learn the truth about your homosexual child, you are afraid to tell anyone else about their shameful secret. You're baffled, hurt, and disappointed. You're ready to tell your kid:

WE'VE BEEN THROUGH SO MUCH TOGETHER,
AND MOST OF IT WAS YOUR FAULT.
Ashleigh Brilliant, Pot-shot
#1336 ©1987.

Many parents assume naively that Christian families just don't have this sort of thing happen to THEM. When parents learn their child is gay, they try to cover it up, which only causes them to be devoid of support. They have been taught that Christians are supposed to be immune to things like this, so their pride keeps them from reaching out for help.

Right along with these feelings, parents may feel God has let them down. After all, they tried. They did all the right things, but God seems to have forsaken them, so they do the worst thing possible: They pull into a shell and keep quiet, refusing to seek help.

But retreating into isolation isn't the answer. Yesterday we had a whopper of a windstorm—they're called "Santa Anas" in California—with dust blowing everywhere. It was difficult to even see the road ahead, but because we had to get out to do some errands, we went anyway. Coping with the windstorms of our lives gets us used to adversity. But those who hide in the storm cellar, so to speak, do very poorly in the storm because they haven't learned how to cope.

Again and again I see folks who have had a lot of difficulties in life coming to a certain degree of acceptance. It just depends on how many times life puts you in the tumbler. You can come out crushed, or you can come out polished. Some people are like diamonds. They know what they're going through is part of life, and they can accept it with incredible calm.

And right along with this, we shouldn't protect our kids from the windstorms of life either. If we shield them from the storms, we rob them of the polishing process that is needed in their lives. If we always rescue our kids from the pain and harshness of life, we make it too soft for them. As someone said:

THE SOFTER WE MAKE IT FOR OUR KIDS
THE HARDER THE LIFE THEY WILL HAVE.

When our kids hit bottom, we just can't always go in and RESCUE them. We can't always pay their rent and FIX things. Sometimes God lets them be in the pigpen for a while to help them get a picture of themselves. Fur-lining the pigpen and making it all better delays the work the Lord may be doing in their lives—to bring them to themselves. As someone said:

PAIN PLANTS THE FLAG OF REALITY
IN THE FORTRESS OF A REBEL HEART.

Parents Must Come Out of the Closet Too

Yes, our dreams for our children are broken, but we are not without hope. Almost every day I hear from parents who have finally realized that they can't let an abscess continue festering because it will poison their entire being. They see the truth in the slogan:

WE ARE ONLY AS SICK AS OUR SECRETS.

They realize you get bitter, wrinkled, and old if you don't open up about your pain. When we can drain our abscesses, healing will begin.

To anyone who is "too embarrassed to talk about it," I can only say that if you will come out of that closet and share with at least one other person, it will be like turning on a tiny light in utter darkness. And, you just may be surprised about how well you will be accepted. Homosexuality used to be a "secret sin," but today it's as common as the word AIDS.

Don't let embarrassment, shame, guilt, fear . . . or pride . . . keep you in the dark closet. Take a chance. Risk it. Come out! You will be amazed at how relieved you will feel. And even if you share with someone and it boomerangs—you are made to feel guilty and "not a very good Christian parent"—it will still be worth the effort. Keep trying. Eventually you will find an understanding heart.

Keep your eyes and ears open. You might even pick up a casual remark made at the beauty shop or in the market or at the dentist's office—something about someone with a gay child or someone who has a son with AIDS. Try to get that person's name and phone number and make contact. As you talk, you will soon be able to detect if this parent is, indeed, experiencing the same problem you have and if he or she has credentials "earned" by surviving the heat of the furnace.

Folks with credentials are a big reason, perhaps, why Spatula is so successful. In Spatula groups around the country, we have parents who have SURVIVED. They are overcomers and are able to help others who have fallen. As Solomon said:

IF ONE FALLS DOWNS,
HIS FRIEND CAN HELP HIM UP.

BUT PITY THE MAN WHO FALLS
AND WHO HAS NO ONE TO PICK HIM UP![1]

What a Support Group Can Do for You

When I was left with feelings of depression over Larry's dis-
appearance into the gay life, I had no support group; that's why
I promised the Lord if I ever got through my dilemma I would
start one for parents who were dying on the vine as I was.
That was a lot to promise, but because I thought I was going
to die from all the stress anyway, I thought I wouldn't really
have to keep it!

One of the practical reasons to be in a support group is that
it will be your sounding board to help you understand your
own emotional blocks. The support group is your setting for
opening up your painful abscess as you look objectively at
your feelings, especially the conflicts you have, and allow others
to reflect back what they are hearing you say and share how
they have coped with their own situations.

The support group also gives you other ideas for coping that
will help you relate to your wayward child. Soon the pain of
humiliation is replaced by strength and forgiveness. You begin
to think, *I CAN get out of this pit of discouragement!*

Of course, support groups aren't magic wands that provide
an "instant fix." Just because you get into a group doesn't
guarantee your child will suddenly come back to the fold. In
the parable of the Prodigal Son, he returned when he was
ready—"when he came to his senses."[2] Any restoration with
your wayward child is within God's timing and control. The
following letter from a Spatula mom puts it in perspective:

> When my husband and I were in the lowest point in our
> hurting, you were there with encouragement that we will
> never forget. I couldn't get over the fact that you even called
> me one evening just to see how things were going for us.
> I will never forget the kind words of guidance you spoke
> to me that night. You said, "IT'S YOUR RESPONSIBILITY

TO LOVE YOUR SON, AND IT'S GOD'S RESPONSIBIL-
ITY TO *CHANGE HIM*. KEEP THE PORCH LIGHT
BURNING BRIGHT." We have done just that, and he does
come home and calls us at least once a week. Time or space
will not allow me to give you the details of all that has
happened, but we are thanking the Lord every day that He
has allowed us to let our son know that we love him!

This mom captured the ambivalence parents feel as they
wait. But while you are in God's waiting room, you will feel the
stirrings of new beginnings as you gain insight through your
journey into wholeness. We know there is no microwave matu-
rity. Becoming whole takes time, and in fact, we are always in
the process of becoming. We never arrive. This is particularly
true of the Christian life, which is a long pilgrimage. So we follow the Lord wherever He leads, because:

WE ARE PILGRIMS, NOT SETTLERS.

When You Survive, Share!

I'm not the only one who's sold on support groups. Letters
come from folks who have been survivors and now want to
pull others out of their pain. For example:

What joy your book has given me! I've ordered more for
the Sunday school class I teach, and we are going to need
still more! My twin daughters share a variety of problems:
one has an emotional disorder and the other is an alco-
holic. The pain associated with emotional disorders and
drug addiction—and a family that doesn't want to believe
these diagnoses—seems overwhelmingly painful.

I have such strong feelings about laughter and joy. . . .
I have seen it work such wonders in others' lives, my own
children included . . .

- - - - - - -

Through you, your writing, and your laughter, God has set
me free . . . I've learned to relax, smile, and even laugh

at my past. . . . Since I was a little girl, I've been through a lot: abandoned, molested, and addicted before I was even an adult; then I got pregnant and was pushed into a bad marriage. Before I turned 30 I'd had three kids, a hysterectomy, and an employer who hurt me with broken promises and heartbreaking lies.

My dream has always been to find some ministry to help people like me. I feel as though I know you and I love what I know. You didn't just write a book that told people how to handle things. You showed all of us the times that you as a Christian felt and handled something poorly, and that made you human to us.

– – – – – – –

It is certainly more fun to give than to receive! I am not forgetting your help when I was at the dungeon's bottom. Today my daily prayer is, "Lord, don't let me forget where I've been!" I look for others in the dungeon and try to give them a similar boost.

All of the above letters reflect the same message: Your suffering should not be wasted. Use what you have learned as you reach out from your heart and pull others along!

NEVER WASTE YOUR PAIN!

Dear Lord...
    Please grant that I shall
    Never waste my pain; for . . .
    To fail without learning,
    To fall without getting up,
    To sin without overcoming,
    To be hurt without forgiving,
    To be discontent without improving,
    To be crushed without becoming more caring,
    To suffer without growing more sensitive,
    Makes of suffering a senseless, futile exercise,
    A tragic loss,
    And of pain,
    The greatest waste of all.
                                    Dick Innes[3]

Whatever kind of devastating blow you've survived, now you have your CREDENTIALS. As you share your experiences, it will be like a healing balm to others who are trying to find their way.

Remember Scripture's promise that we ourselves are refreshed as we refresh others (Prov. 11:25), and GO FOR IT! Find a support group, or better yet, start a support group for parents who are not as far along in their long journey of healing as you are. There are so many hurting folks out there who would benefit from what you have learned by surviving your own ordeal. Some other wise words from Solomon are these:

> Though one may be overpowered,
> two can defend themselves.
> A cord of three strands is not quickly broken.[4]

There are different ways to interpret that verse, but when Solomon talks about three strands, I believe he's talking about you, the person you come alongside to help, AND THE LORD. When you weave a cord like that, it is indestructible.

Remember that sharing your insights will be like making it indelible for you. The lessons you've learned will never fade, and as you continue to refresh others, you will continue to heal as well. I like the way one mom put it:

> I am sorry so many people are suffering because children choose this lifestyle, but you have the only answer—and that is to love them anyway. Actually, that is the answer to any situation unless I want to become a recluse. There have been times when I felt like doing just that. But I need friends and interaction with people. I've always said when I find a perfect friend I will give up all the rest. I'm grateful my friends tolerate me.

When you no longer need the support group, you'll know it. Usually the best clue is that you start wanting to help others as you have been helped. And then you can move on to the second stage of your healing. Helping others will continue to help you because their gratitude is so very nourishing. We all need to feel that we matter to someone. Caring for others can help break the stranglehold that self- centeredness has on us. Showing compassion for new friends refocuses our attention outside ourselves so that feelings of warmth return to us. I like to say:

FRIENDSHIP DOUBLES OUR JOYS
AND DIVIDES OUR SORROWS.

When Larry disappeared into the gay lifestyle for the second time, I had learned my lesson. Instead of going into isolation as I had the first time, I began leading a support group, and for the next several years that gave me support in turn.

On Mother's Day, 1986, Larry came back home to tell us he had felt conviction about his life and wanted our forgiveness. That was a huge splash of joy, but perhaps an even bigger splash came when he and I were interviewed on the "Focus on the Family" radio program. During that interview Larry called me his "BEST FRIEND." I will always be Larry's mother, but for him to call me his best friend was a high tribute. I like to say:

MOTHER BY CHANCE . . . FRIEND BY CHOICE.

Being Larry's best friend means more than being Number One in anything else.

It Pays to Have Friends in All the Right Places

This chapter on friendship has to include an experience I had recently when I needed to have eye surgery—a cataract extraction with a lens implant. That was the bad news, but the good news was that my surgeon would be the same ophthalmologist who had taken care of Bill twenty-six years before when I had found him lying on a mountain road up in San Gabriel Canyon. Dr. Robb Hicks was the same one who had gone with us to the Veterans Administration offices to confirm Bill's medical condition for disability coverage.

Over the years Bill and I would see him for yearly checkups and he is the kind of person who, when you bring in a cartoon or joke to share, always says, "Oh, is this for ME?" And then he dashes off to make copies of it to put on the bulletin board for his staff. Through the years we've become good friends, and actually, we're on a first-name basis, but I hesitate to call him "Robb." "Dr. Hicks" sounds a lot more professional for a successful ophthalmologist.

The night before my surgery was scheduled, a call came from the anesthesiologist who would be part of my surgical team the next day. He asked some routine questions, getting additional history and checking to see if I had any allergies. Then he said, "Now, once we get STARTED we don't stop for ANYTHING. So, if you have to go to the bathroom, just go ahead as the surgery is taking place."

I was shocked, but he assured me that lots of OLDER people had this problem. I let him know I wasn't even on Medicare YET and made a mental note to make sure I wouldn't drink anything for HOURS before I went in, just to be *sure*.

Finally, he said, "Well, I think you're all set for surgery tomorrow morning on your right eye . . ."

"My RIGHT eye? No, no!" I told him. "It's my LEFT eye!"

"Oh," he said. "I guess the surgical schedule is incorrect. Wait. Here, I've got it on another list. Yes, I see it is the *left* eye. Well, see you in the morning!"

Happy that we made THAT clarification, I tried to get some sleep, but it took a long time to drop off. The anesthesiologist's words, "Once we're started we can't stop," whirled around in my head. What if I did have to go? What if we had an earthquake and the power went out? After all, they said they couldn't stop for ANYTHING! What if I had to sneeze or cough?

One Size Does NOT Fit All

Bill drove me to the hospital EARLY the next morning. I was taken back to a small dressing room where I was told to remove my clothes and put on the classic hospital gown. The gown ended above my knees and was so skimpy it didn't even meet in the back. And even if the sides did meet, it only had one string, so I couldn't have tied it if I'd wanted to! Considering the high prices hospitals charge, it would seem that gowns could at least have *two* strings to tie. Then the nurse asked for my shoe size. I wondered whatever for, and she replied, "So we will get the right size booties for you."

I couldn't help but think, *All this just for EYE SURGERY!*

Finally, I had on my skimpy gown with one string missing in the back, and my fuzzy booties. Then they laid me out on a padded steel table, waiting to go into surgery. A nurse came in and put a little paper hat on me that completely covered my hair. Because she had read my books, she joked that there wouldn't be any geranium in my hat, but I'd have to make the best of it. Another nurse came in to place a pillow under my knees, which was comforting. Then they wheeled me into the operating room.

Dr. Hicks told me they were going to put an oxygen mask over my face and would give me just enough anesthetic to keep me in a sort of half-conscious twilight zone—they didn't want me to go completely out during the operation. But if I started to feel pain, all I had to say was "MORE," and the anesthesiologist would oblige.

That's fine, I thought to myself, *but how will they hear me through the oxygen mask?* Oh well, that was the least of my worries. I still remembered what the anesthesiologist had said on the phone the night before. I began thinking about how much I didn't want to go to the bathroom, but you know how *that* works. Have you ever thought how much you didn't want to do something—until that was ALL you could think of?

I just wanted to be OUT of there and wake up when it was over, but that wasn't the way it worked. My eye was propped open with some sort of tool, but I couldn't feel anything. I felt like I was floating but I could still hear the doctor and nurses talking. Dr. Hicks was saying, "This is a SPECIAL lady. Years ago I worked on her husband, who had been listed in critical condition from an accident in the mountains. Then she lost a son, and then another son . . ."

At this point I almost interrupted him, but I guess I was too groggy. I kept thinking, *Oh, no, I don't want to relive my whole story HERE.* But as the doctor went on with the operation he said, "She had another son leave home for many years—to go into the gay lifestyle. She's written many books . . . yes, that looks good. Are you going to get that wire loop there?"

As I kept drifting in and out of consciousness, I heard Dr. Hicks say, "Some time ago I was driving over to USC to teach a class, and I turned on the radio and here was this very special lady we're operating on today, sharing her story. I realized how much God had been blessing her. Somehow hearing her whole story again reminded me that I had been a part of it at the very beginning in this very same hospital so many years ago."

As Dr. Hicks was telling my story, I lay there, not feeling any pain because the side of my head where he was working was completely numb. It gave me new appreciation for the term *numbskull!* Finally, I heard him talk about "closure" and someone taped a shield over my eye. Dr. Hicks took off my oxygen mask and said, "Everything went fine. You're going to be okay."

Then I felt the IV coming out of my arm and a light, moist brush on my cheek. Good grief! Was he crying over my story? Dr. Hicks had left the operating room, so I asked the nurse what had brushed my cheek. She replied, "No, that wasn't a tear. The doctor just gave you a little kiss before he left the room, and said, 'This is for a special lady.'"

My heart was smiling as I realized how thankful I was—for NOT having to go to the bathroom . . . that there HADN'T been an earthquake . . . that the anesthesia HAD worked its magic and kept the pain away . . . and that the nurses had been so CARING. Above all, I was thankful for my doctor, who was more than a skilled surgeon. He was a good friend, and good friends are hard to find. As one of my favorite poems puts it:

> Friendship is a Priceless Gift
> that cannot be bought or sold,
> But its value is far greater
> than a mountain made of gold—

For gold is cold and lifeless,
       it can neither see nor hear,
And in the time of trouble
       it is powerless to cheer—
       It has no ears to listen,
No heart to understand,
       It cannot bring you comfort
            or reach out a helping hand—
So when you ask
       God for a GIFT,
            Be thankful if HE sends
Not diamonds, pearls or riches,
       but the love of real true friends.
                                        Helen Steiner Rice[5]

I've included this chapter on friends because I know how valuable they can be. Friends are the ones with whom you can share, confess faults, cry—yes, and above all, *laugh*. I've had more laughs with good friends than anyone, and why not? After all:

A FRIEND IS ONE WHO KNOWS ALL ABOUT YOU
AND LOVES YOU ANYWAY.

Bugaboo Busters

LOVE IS WARM ARMS
INSTEAD OF COLD SHOULDERS.

If a lion's roar isn't getting you anyplace,
try a bear hug.

FRIENDS MAY COME AND FRIENDS MAY GO,
BUT ENEMIES ACCUMULATE.[6]

TRY A QUICK HUG TO
COOL A SLOW BURN.

Grudges are like hand grenades:
It's wise to release them before they destroy you.

Some folks cause happiness wherever they go,
others whenever they go.

From the Spatula mailbag:
God bless you . . . as my well gets deeper
and darker, you are the light.

Your books tell how I feel, and that means a lot. I didn't think I would find anyone who knew how I felt.

How wonderful it was to hear from you and know that someone really cared that my life was in a heap around my feet.

INSOMUCH AS ANYONE
PUSHES YOU NEARER TO GOD,
HE OR SHE IS YOUR FRIEND.

Sympathy is YOUR pain in MY heart.

It is one of the most beautiful compensations of life that no one can sincerely try to help another without helping herself.

FORGIVE YOUR ENEMIES,
BUT NEVER FORGET THEIR NAMES!

Message in a fortune cookie:
  You appeal to a small select group of con-
  fused people.

A true friend is always loyal." (Prov. 17:17 TLB)

6

If the Sky Falls Tomorrow, Have Clouds for Breakfast*

*I*s it true that anyone can learn to develop a positive attitude no matter what comes into her life? Going through my mail every week, I sometimes wonder how that works when so many folks have stories that are anything but positive. Just a sampling of phrases from their letters will show you what I mean:

> This morning, on my way to visit my son in jail for second-degree murder . . .

> I have two children recovering from chemical dependencies, and my concerns about their sexual orientation would fill a book . . .

> My heart cries when I listen to unsuspecting friends make jokes about gays, queers, etc., but I don't say a word. I *love* my son and I *need* my friends! . . .

> Our precious son died as the result of being run off the road by an unidentified driver who fled the scene . . .

---

* Adapted from Cooper Edens, *If You're Afraid of the Dark, Remember the Night Rainbow* (La Jolla, Calif.: Green Tiger Press, 1979).

I have an eighteen-year-old daughter who has been diag-
nosed as being mentally handicapped. We go through a lot
of criticism because people and family expect her to per-
form like she's eighteen and she's not able to do that . . .

My husband accidentally ran over our six-year-old grandson with the tractor our grandson adored—and had
sneaked away to watch. He died on the way to the hospital.
We are still heartbroken and hurt that God would allow
this to happen . . .

I could go on listing comments from letter after letter—
enough to fill a book. The obstacles life throws in the path of
some people are beyond belief. Is it possible for these folks to
be positive? *Yes!* I know it is because many of these same people
have shared with me how they have survived and triumphed,
despite the obstacles.

The truth is, we all encounter obstacles as we try to reach
our goals in life. I call them roadblocks to happiness, and
sometimes they can seem unsurmountable. At other times
they can threaten to destroy our very existence. The key to
handling road blocks is to be flexible in making changes. As
we become skilled in dealing with roadblocks, these hurdles
can become helpers instead. They can be like engines that pro-
pel us toward our goals. I love the saying:

AN OBSTACLE IS LIKE THE HURDLE IN
A STEEPLECHASE:
RIDE UP TO IT, THROW YOUR HEART OVER IT,
AND THE HORSE WILL GO ALONG TOO!

The key to shifting your attitude into positive gear is to re-
think how you look at things. As children, we were trained to
see obstacles as just that—hurdles that were in our way, problems with no answers. Being young, we didn't know the difference between what was new and harmful and what was
new and exciting. We were warned to avoid many things, to
be cautious, to stick with what was safe and comfortable.
When we reached adulthood, we kept this same philosophy

and became frozen in old patterns of response. Let's look at those familiar patterns and analyze how they affect us.

Fear Can Help You Do Your Best

A major obstacle for most of us is FEAR, that little darkroom where negatives are developed. But the positive side is that fear provides the energy to do your best in a new situation. When you're afraid, your senses sharpen, your eyes narrow, you pump adrenaline, and you are able to focus with more energy. You become more AWARE. A mother of three small children wrote:

> I would like to tell you how I once again was blessed by your books. Today I had to have a test that showed a problem with my left kidney—a *tumor*, which I choose to believe is benign until I hear differently.
> Anyway, last night was real difficult for me. I was scared to death of going for the test today, not so much for me but for my kids (age eight, two, and six months). I just couldn't imagine having to say good-bye to them.
> Then I remembered your books. I pulled out *Geranium* and *Splashes of Joy* and read excerpts from both. I read all the things I had highlighted when I read them the first time. Today I said the verse from Isaiah 26:3 several times as I waited for the procedure to begin. I did not feel peace immediately, and not nearly as much as I hoped for, but I had something to focus on, *something positive*. I thank you so much.

I know where this mom is coming from. When my doctor first told me I had diabetes, he gave me restrictions and limitations I had to live with each day. Fear clutched at my heart because it was all so demanding and seemed to be an overwhelming challenge I couldn't meet. But because I knew that God's grace would be sufficient for me, I was able to settle into the new routine, and as I made the changes necessary to live my new lifestyle, my fears subsided.

When we're afraid to do something but do it anyway, we soon realize that fear is working to our advantage—and even projecting us into action. After doing whatever scares us, we realize it wasn't so bad after all. Actually, it was kind of fun! Conquering fear can be a worthwhile learning adventure instead of an ordeal.

You can't, however, make the jump directly from fear to triumph. You have to go through that "in-between" stage. You have to deal with feeling uncomfortable in new situations, new jobs, new challenges, whatever it is that frightens you. But you learn to adjust to it and go THROUGH it. So it's not comfortable. So what? As someone supposedly observed,

WHO SAID LIFE IS SUPPOSED TO BE COMFORTABLE?

"You'll Be Fine—Just FINE!"

Recently I went in for a routine medical checkup. As usual, the nurse ushered me into one of those little examining rooms where I lay on the cold, hard table with the white slippery paper on it, waiting for the doctor to come in. As I waited, I stared at an anatomy chart on the wall, trying not to listen to conversations that drifted in from the hallway. Evidently, my doctor was on the phone and I could hear him saying, "Oh, you'll be fine . . . you'll be just fine!" I wondered how he could be so sure of that, but his firm, confident voice assured the caller that he or she would "be just fine."

A few minutes went by, and I began leafing through an old, outdated magazine. Then I heard voices again and the sound of tapping, made by an older person with a cane, perhaps. I pictured the doctor with his arm around some old fellow as he walked him to the door. Then I heard his voice again saying, "Why, yes, Joe, you'll be fine . . . you'll be just fine!"

In a couple of minutes, the doctor finally poked his head into the room where I was waiting and said cheerfully, "Well, Kiddo, how are you doing today?"

(Although I am old enough to be his mother, he calls me "Kiddo"—probably to make me feel younger.)

My response was, "Well, it really doesn't matter how I am doing TODAY, because I know that I WILL BE FINE, JUST FINE!"

Then we laughed together as I told him how I had overheard him give two other patients that same line as if it were a part of his treatment.

He gave me my usual exam and then talked about the results of some tests I had taken earlier. We chatted a little longer, and then, as I was leaving, he added, "You're going to be fine—just fine!"

Walking out to the car, I couldn't help but chuckle. And then I wondered . . . *Perhaps "You'll be fine" WAS or IS part of his treatment.* I had to admit those simple words had caused my heart to smile and soothed my troubled spirit. It reminded me of Proverbs 16:24 (NIV), "Pleasant words are a honeycomb, / sweet to the soul, and healing to the bones."

I decided I was thankful for my doctor's positive attitude. Instead of some gloomy prognosis, I much preferred the confidence of knowing I'd be "just fine." What a difference a few words can make! For example, how do these negative phrases make you feel?

> I can't . . .
> It's a hassle . . .
> Life's a battle . . .
> If only . . .
> What can I do now?

Now look at the following phrases, which contain positive, strengthening words:

> I can do it . . .
> This has possibilities after all . . .
> Life is full of opportunities . . .
> I learned something from that . .
> There is nothing God and I can't handle together.

Words *do* have power, so use them carefully!

Let the Good Times Roll!

Bad times come to all of us, and it amazes me how, for some people, they seem to come *one right after the other*.

One mother wrote to say she sympathizes with those who go through pain because she'd had her share continuously. Her daughter had been in and out of hospitals due to mental illness. Her son had dropped out of school, become addicted to drugs, and moved in with his pregnant girlfriend, who already had another child. Her husband, who had used alcohol to escape the turbulent home life, died of cancer at the age of forty-nine. One bright spot was that her husband made a confession of faith before he died, but this woman's problems have continued. When her son's girlfriend left him, the mother took him and the baby in, but the son stayed out all night, slept most of the day, and helped very little with the baby. When she asked him to leave, he retaliated by saying that she could no longer see her grandchild. She admitted:

> I am bewildered, and I feel a lack of support and real understanding from others, including Christians. I go to groups that help while I'm there, but am I expecting too much from others and allowing myself to slip into negativity and self-pity? I still can't rise above all this. . . . I do a lot of crying and feel desperate a lot of the time.

This mom has many feelings, but one of the major ones is discouragement. When we are discouraged, we lose heart and fear creeps in. So overcoming *dis*couragement is simply a matter of taking away the *DIS* and adding the *EN*. To do this, you have to be ready to choose your dream—and run with it. Hearten yourself to *do*, not just to *wish*.

Another mom's letter tells of a Mother's Day when her only son informed her he was a homosexual. He admitted living in a house with three other gay men. The mother tried to stay calm on the outside, but on the inside she was falling apart.

As her son left, she told him she loved him and would pray for him. She walked to a friend's house nearby and collapsed into her friend's arms, sobbing. She felt her world was crashing down—again.

Her husband, a counselor, had died two months earlier, and a year before that, her daughter had been killed in a car crash. Her son was the only family she had left, and now she felt she had lost him too.

Since that shocking Mother's Day, this mom has made progress by reading about homosexuality and talking with close friends and her pastor, who is the only one in her church who knows. She walks the tightrope, trying to demonstrate love and acceptance for her son and his friend while maintaining her own standards. She wrote:

> The last few months have alternately been painful, difficult, encouraging, filled with God's strength and hope for my son, and at other times filled with my own depression. I've discovered I have had many of the same emotions and physical reactions I did when my daughter was killed!
>
> I am trying very much to keep my eyes fixed on God, His faithfulness, and His great power, and asking Him to: (1) fill my heart anew each day with *His* love for my son and his friend (I've discovered *my* love ebbs and flows!), (2) work mightily in my son's heart and life, (3) help me be sensitive to the leading of His spirit and rely on His wisdom and not my emotions and impatience, and (4) to use all this for my growth, His glory, and the help and encouragement of other hurting parents.

This mom is a survivor and a winner because she realizes her love ebbs and flows, but God's love is unchanging. She's having to make adjustments because bad times do that. We all are dealing with ever-changing times. As somebody said, "Constant change is here to stay. The world changes so fast you couldn't stay wrong all the time if you tried!"

While change will always be with us, it is not a popular concept. Everybody is in favor of progress, but few of us welcome change. Some people continually change jobs, mates, and friends, but they never think of changing themselves, and they stagnate. Everyone has a personal list of excuses that can lead to stagnation. Here is mine:

1. I've always done it this way. Why change now?
2. I'm not ready to try that.
3. Who needs it? I'm doing all right.
4. I tried that, and it was uncomfortable.

5. I can't afford to take the time.
6. That's not my job.
7. That won't work—it just "ain't me."

Whenever I hear myself using any of the above excuses, I stop and ask:
"What are you trying to avoid?"
"Are you getting lazy or complacent?"
"What do you need to do to make sure you keep growing and changing?"

When bad times or problems of any kind smack you, remember: You have a choice. You can see nothing but grief and gloomees, or you can see opportunities to make things better.

ALL SOME PEOPLE NEED TO MAKE THEM HAPPY IS
A CHANGE,
AND MOST OF THE TIME THAT'S ALL A BABY
NEEDS TOO!

Do You See Obstacles or Opportunities?

Opportunities come in all shapes and sizes. What if those things you see now as obstacles could be seen instead as GOLD BRICKS? Bricks can be used to build a wall or as paving stones for your road to success. You can follow the yellow brick road to where you want to be, or you can remain stymied by that big wall that seals off any progress you want to make. *It all depends on how you look at the obstacles.*

You may have seen one of those drawings where the instructions ask you if you see a young girl or an old woman. If you look at the drawing one way, you will see a young girl. Look at it from a little different angle, and you will see an old woman.

The point is that perspective is all about how we choose to see things. Because we look as much with our mind as with our eyes, we tend to "see" what we expect to see or want to see. Changing our perspective calls for a *willingness to see things differently.* That's the key to developing a positive attitude regardless of what happens to us.

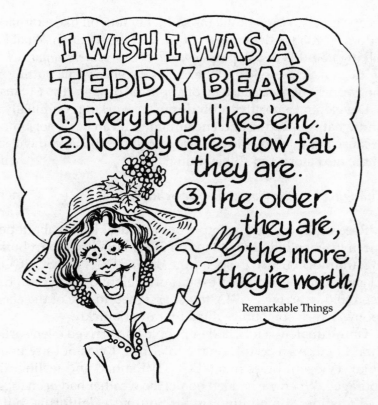

While I was working on this book, Southern California was devastated by the most extensive wildfires in history. Several people died, thousands of acres were blackened, and hundreds of homes were destroyed or damaged. One of the hardest-hit areas was Laguna Beach, but one man whose house had burned to the ground kept a positive attitude. He said:

"I'M LOOKING AT THE BRIGHT SIDE.
I GOT RID OF THOSE DARN TERMITES!"

When you talk about the power of perspective, it's important to refer to positive ATTITUDE, not positive THINKING. There is a BIG difference between the two. A lot of folks tell me that the "power of positive thinking" doesn't work for them because it seems to suggest that you have to stick your head in the sand to escape reality. When problems suddenly hit you like a tornado, it does no good to deny the seriousness of the situation. What I'm talking about is developing a *positive, God-centered approach to life* that takes the good and the bad as it comes while putting on the garment of praise instead of a spirit of despair (Isa. 61:3 TLB).

Developing a positive attitude means working continually to find what is uplifting and encouraging. It can be done; I know because I've made a study of being positive, and as you will see in the next story, I'm still learning!

Changing Perspective at Traffic School

Recently I received a simple but practical lesson about perspective when Bill dropped me off at the Fullerton Court Building around 7:00 A.M. to spend the day at TRAFFIC SCHOOL. Classes weren't supposed to start until eight o'clock, but I had been told to arrive EARLY to get assigned to one of the classrooms, which sometimes filled up rather quickly.

Unfortunately, a lot of other people had arrived even earlier than I had. As a result, I have to admit, I was not my usual POSITIVE self. I was in a NEGATIVE mood and feeling discouraged. When we had left home, the weather had been foggy and misting, something rare for Southern California, but it seemed to go with the rest of my day. By the time I came up the walk to the court building it had already started to rain. My gloom increased when I saw a long, straggly line of folks under black umbrellas that stretched for almost a block down the side of the building. They were all waiting for the door to open so they could get registered for traffic school.

Later I learned that *four hundred people* were there that day, eager to spend eight hours being instructed in the horrors of auto accidents caused by careless driving. (Also, they wanted to avoid having their tickets go on their driving records, not to mention getting their insurance rates increased.)

As I joined the long, soggy line, I recalled again how I had gotten my ticket—for doing sixty-five miles per hour in what I thought was a fifty-five zone. On that particular day, I was in positive spirits, looking forward to sharing my story with several hundred women at a speaking engagement, so it was easy to decide that "Whatever, Lord," applied to ALL aspects of life. I smiled and actually THANKED the officer as I signed the speeding ticket.

It's one thing, though, to feel positive when you get a ticket; it's another to have to get up early on a rainy Saturday morning to spend your ENTIRE DAY at traffic school! And standing in that long, soggy line of big black umbrellas didn't help either. (*Why is it*, I wondered, *that everyone in Southern California seems to have a BIG BLACK umbrella?*)

Have We Got a Class for You!

When I finally got to the door, there sat a lady who was signing people in and directing them to various classrooms. It was then that I learned that almost all the room assignments had already been made.

"Let's see," she murmured. "The classrooms are really full . . . I hope we can squeeze you in. But first, may I please see your driver's license?"

I produced my license and with maybe a hint of irritation in my voice asked why that was necessary. Wasn't the copy of my traffic ticket and my notice to appear in traffic school sufficient?

"Some violators—particularly professional people—try to hire people to sit in for them at traffic school," she explained patiently. "We just have to check every license to be sure the person coming to traffic school is the SAME person who got the ticket!"

"Did you say all the classes were full?" I asked anxiously. "Isn't there any room left at ALL?"

"There is one special class where I think we can fit you in. It's primarily for motorcyclists, but we had a couple of other women who couldn't get into the regular classes. You can go into this group in room 208 and still get your credit for attending."

I told her whatever she had was good enough for me. Actually, I was thankful to get into ANY group after waiting an HOUR outside in the rain.

In an even MORE negative mood than when I had left home, I hurried down the hallway and finally found room 208. I opened the door, and even though I knew this was a class of "bikers," I wasn't prepared for what I saw. There were at least 200 guys crammed into a room that was built to hold no more than 175. Everywhere I looked I saw red plaid bandannas, grubby, bushy beards, sleeveless T-shirts sporting vulgar phrases, tattoos that were even more graphic than the T-shirts, black leather jackets, and heavy, greasy boots. The windowless room was hot, and the air conditioning was *definitely* not working. The odor that hit me seemed to be a cross between a pig farm and a glue factory.

I finally did see a couple of "normal-looking" women like myself, but they were sitting way up in the front. There was no way to sit by them anyway because all those seats were taken. After stepping gingerly over several pairs of big boots, I found an empty chair.

Next to me on my right was a huge, bearded biker with tattoos on both arms. He wore a red-plaid bandanna headband, and his long, stringy hair hung almost to his shoulders. Gaudy rings sparkled on his fingers, and he had another red bandanna in his hand. It looked as if he had been using it to wipe the grease off his motorcycle, but as I watched he wiped the perspiration from his face! Then he put it down on his knee and let it dangle there, ready for quick use when he needed it again.

On the other side of me was an incredible hulk with a protruding belly, gigantic boots, and even bigger tattoos than the first biker. At his feet was a helmet with insignias all over it, including at least two swastikas.

It was a motley crowd, to say the least! The old saying, "I wouldn't want to meet either of these guys in a dark alley" came to mind. Actually, I wasn't too crazy about meeting them in traffic school either!

"I'm Looking for a Few Good Students!"

Feeling as though my day had not started on a very positive note, I tried to slump low in my chair and be unnoticed by all the bikers around me. Then our teacher walked in. He looked and sounded like a drill instructor from nearby Camp Pendleton. No wonder. The first thing he told us was that he was an ex-marine and a California Highway Patrol officer, and he wasn't going to take ANY guff from anyone.

"All right! Listen up, everybody," he growled. "There will be NO sleeping in my class, NO writing notes, NO reading, and NO asking to use the phone out in the hall. You will not be allowed to go to the bathroom until we break for lunch. Don't try to slip out when I'm not looking because there's a marshal posted just outside the door who will nail you in a second. Anyone who smarts off will have to leave, and that means losing credit for traffic school."

Then, with obvious relish, our instructor told us about one guy who had gone to school all day and at 4:30, just before dismissal time, he had smarted off and been dismissed with no credit at all. Our instructor knew exactly why we were there—to spend the whole day in order to eliminate the ticket penalty. We were in his clutches for the next eight hours, and we had to act like model prisoners every second!

Except for a brief lunch break, we spent ALL DAY squashed into that hot, crowded room with NO AIR CONDITIONING. None of us wanted to be there, but we had no choice as we listened to our ex-marine instructor enthusiastically spew out the facts about traffic mayhem. We learned far more than we wanted to know, including the difference between a one-point and a two-point violation and how many points it took to lose your driver's license. And, of course, there were the films—one about defensive driving and another showing what happens when people operate automobiles recklessly. Finally the moment came for our "graduation."

I Thought I Could Remain Anonymous, But . . .

As the instructor called out our names in his loud, raspy voice, we all had to march forward one by one to accept our "diplomas"—the certificates proving that we had finished traffic school, assuring us that our record would now be cleared.

Finally the instructor came to my name and said in a booming voice: "BARBARA ELIZABETH JOHNSON." (Somehow, it
reminded me of when I was a little girl. The only times I had
heard my middle name used was when my mother was upset
with me.)

Feeling very official and wondering why they weren't playing
"Pomp and Circumstance," I made my way forward to receive
my certificate. Smiling at our instructor, I took the coveted piece
of paper and turned quickly to leave. After spending eight mis-
erable hours in a hot, smelly room with people who weren't my
kind of crowd, I just wanted to get out of there FAST. *At least,* I
thought, *in THIS bunch, there's no chance of meeting anybody who
knows me.*

Wrong! As I whizzed by one of the other "normal-looking"
ladies, she jumped up and grabbed me, almost screaming,
"BARBARA JOHNSON! I've read all your books, and I'm just
SO happy to finally meet you."

There was nothing I could do, nowhere to run. The woman
had me in a bear hug, and I was trapped. I think Moses said,
"You may be sure your sin will find you out."[1] Well, Moses certainly was one who should know. He'd been nailed after murder-
ing an Egyptian and hiding him in the sand. But I hadn't
murdered anybody. I had just driven a little too fast without
meaning to. Wasn't it Murphy who dreamed up the law that
says, "If anything can go wrong, it will"? Just then, with all those
bikers glaring at me, I thought of Johnson's Rule of Thumb:

GO TO TRAFFIC SCHOOL,
AND SOMEONE WILL RECOGNIZE YOU.

Oh, well, I decided to make the best of it. Hiding my embarrassment as best I could, I told her that anybody who loves my
books is my instant friend and we chatted on the way out of
traffic school. It turned out that she was from a nearby church
pastored by a prominent minister I knew.

"I hope you don't plan to tell your pastor you saw me at
traffic school," I said with a laugh.

"Oh, I won't," she assured me. "I don't particularly want him to know *I've* been here either."

I Learned Several Lessons That Day

Just then Bill drove up. I said good-bye to my new friend and climbed into the car. As we drove along, I was quiet for several miles, thinking about what I had learned on a foggy, rainy day in a hot, smelly traffic-school room. Yes, I had seen some graphic pictures of bloodied people being pulled out of crumpled masses of metal, and I had been reminded of how dangerous a car can be, but that wasn't my only lesson. My other teachers had been a motley crew of bikers and one nice, "normal-looking" lady who had identified me just as I had been hoping to remain ANONYMOUS.

Yes, my sin had found me out, and I thought of some other bits of Scripture like, "Do not think of yourself more highly than you ought" and, "In humility consider others better than yourselves."[2] I could almost hear Jesus saying, "You know, Barbara, I used to spend a lot of time with folks just like this. I died for them as well as for you."

I winced as I realized my concept of "normal" was pretty snobbish. After all, as Patsy Clairmont says:

NORMAL IS THE SETTING ON A DRYER.[3]

And as I thought of those two big bikers who had sat beside me, another saying came to mind:

IF WE EVER MAKE A MISTAKE IN JUDGMENT,
LET IT BE ON THE SIDE OF MERCY.

Somewhere those two young men had mothers who probably stayed up nights worrying about them. I said a quick prayer for both bikers, especially the guy with the swastikas on his helmet, wishing there were some way I could cover up those ugly symbols with the little Care Bears stickers I love to use on letters.

Those moments of prayer made me feel better. Despite the negative things that had been part of my traffic-school day, I realized there was a lot to be encouraged about after all. For one thing, my penalty was wiped out. Psalm 32:1 came to mind, "What relief for those who have confessed their sins and God has cleared their record" (TLB).

And even though I had been spotted by someone when I didn't want anyone to recognize me, she had turned out to be a cheerful gal. Commiserating together about traffic school reminded me of something opera star Beverly Sills said:

I'm not happy, I'm cheerful. There's a difference. A happy woman has no cares at all. A cheerful woman has cares but has learned how to deal with them.

If you find you're going in the wrong direction... Remember that God allows U-turns.

OPEN our eyes that we may turn from darkness to light ... Acts 26:18

© "Sonshine Promises" created by Gretchen Clasby, Cedar Hill Studio. Used by permission.

Of course there are many problems that are far more serious than having to go to traffic school. I've had a few of those myself, and so have many others, some of whose letters I have shared in this chapter. The point to my traffic-school story is that changing a situation from bad to good, from defeat to victory, usually means changing your attitude and how you look at it. Many times this isn't done while you're driving home. It can take years, but God can fine-tune us for His glory.

One mom wrote to tell of learning that her son was gay while he was a student in a Christian college. Since then many years have passed, but he has stayed in the homosexual lifestyle. This mom's letter continued:

> In these past years our emotions have been on a roller coaster; we have probably experienced every feeling imaginable. I found release and relief much sooner than my husband, for it was only a month ago, during a serious illness and following an overdose of drugs, that our son asked for his dad. At that time they both experienced a wonderful healing and reconciliation.
>
> If it weren't for the grace and strength from God that I receive on a daily basis I could never end this letter by telling you how much I laughed and laughed as I read your book. I don't have the answers, but I DO HAVE GOD!

This dear mom is right. We don't have all the answers but we do have God, and that's why we have the ability to choose between being positive or letting the daily frustrations of life rob our joy. So keep working on an upbeat perspective, and stay ahead of the game by remembering these words from a ninety-five-year-old lady in a rest home:

I GET UP IN THE MORNING,
I PUT MY FEET ON THE FLOOR,
I KNOW WHO I AM,
I KNOW WHAT DAY IT IS,
AND I SAY, "PRAISE THE LORD!"

Bugaboo Busters

A PESSIMIST IS SOMEONE WHO BELIEVES
THAT WHEN HER CUP RUNNETH OVER . . .
SHE'LL NEED A MOP.

WILL THE LAST PERSON OUT OF THE TUNNEL
PLEASE TURN OUT THE LIGHT?

SOME COMPLAIN BECAUSE THE ROSE HAS THORNS;
SOME GIVE THANKS BECAUSE THE THORNS HAVE
ROSES.

From the Spatula mailbag:
    While we who are hurting from situations
    live in the thorns, it's great to read a book that
    leads us to the beauty of a rose at the end of
    the stem. My thanks and appreciation.

FAITH IS SEEING LIGHT WITH YOUR HEART
WHEN ALL YOUR EYES SEE IS THE DARKNESS.

ALPHABET PRAYER

A . . . Almighty God
B . . . Bless my family and me
C . . . Comfort me
D . . . Draw me to You in prayer
E . . . Enlighten me
F . . . Forgive my sins
G . . . Give me a few good friends
H . . . Help me to do Your will
I . . . I am Your servant
J . . . Joyful are my days
K . . . Keep me from harm
L . . . Lead me to still waters
M . . . Make me a vessel of Your love
N . . . Nature is Your masterpiece
O . . . Open new doors for me
P . . . Please, grant me peace of mind
Q . . . Quench my thirst for knowledge
R . . . Reside with me always
S . . . Shield me from danger
T . . . Teach me to love unconditionally
U . . . Use me to inspire others
V . . . Visit me in solitude
W . . . When I fail, lift me up
X . . . XXX's stand for my love for You
Y . . . Your love fills me with gratitude
Z . . . Zestfully, I thank You. Amen.

Evelyn Heinz[4]

IT NEVER HURTS YOUR EYESIGHT
TO LOOK ON THE BRIGHT SIDE OF THINGS.

Positive-Attitude Check List:
____ Fill what's empty.
____ Empty what's full.
____ Scratch where it itches.

MOST PEOPLE ARE WILLING TO CHANGE,
NOT BECAUSE THEY SEE THE LIGHT,
BUT BECAUSE THEY FEEL THE HEAT.

That is why we never give up. Though our bodies are dying, our inner strength in the Lord is growing every day. These troubles and sufferings of ours are, after all, quite small and won't last very long. Yet this short time of distress will result in God's richest blessing upon us forever and ever! So we do not look at what we can see right now, the troubles all around us, but we look forward to the joys in heaven which we have not yet seen. The troubles will soon be over, but the joys to come will last forever. (2 Cor. 4:16–18 TLB)

7

Life Is a Great Big Canvas . . .
Throw All the Paint on It You Can

I'm single," her letter began, "so I don't have any children except for my students. I'm going to try to and 'CHOOSE TO BE HAPPY' and 'LOOK FOR THE JOY.' People think I've lost my mind because I say out loud: 'I'M LOOKING FOR THE JOY!'"

This lady hasn't lost her mind; on the contrary, she's found the secret to getting off the bottom and reaching the top. If you're LOOKING for the joy and CHOOSING to be happy, this chapter is loaded with ideas just for you. Have fun!

Try Celebrating the First of Every Month

A new month is always special to me. I like to celebrate wildly on the first day of the month by changing the bedsheets, taking a leisurely bubble bath, and doing FUN things just for myself. My only problem is that since I've mentioned in other books about how I celebrate the first of each month, folks start calling me at 5:00 A.M. to ask me what I'm doing to celebrate. Then they tell me what THEY are doing.

So the first day of every month I spend most of the morning answering the phone. Last month it was NOON before I even had time to brush my teeth, all because the phone kept ringing with well-wishers who wanted to join me in celebrating the first of the month!

I start looking forward to the new month about a week ahead, planning something simple but FUN to do. Sometimes it's just making a long-distance phone call or dropping a note to someone I love but have not been in touch with for a long time.

No mail gets opened, however; nor do I cook or do anything that is not SPECIAL on the first of the month. Sometimes I try a different hairstyle, or maybe I buy a new pair of earrings. Like everyone else, I get stacks of catalogs and other advertisements during the month and never have time to go through them. Sometimes on the first of the month I unplug the phone, get real comfy, and "shop" via catalog.

The first is one day that is SPECIAL for me. No one is pulling or tugging at me about a deadline. No one is demanding my time. It is MY DAY to pamper myself, and boy, have I learned how to do that!

On one recent first-of-the-month I drove up on a high bluff overlooking the freeway, parked, and just sat there watching all the activity below. I put on a super new Gaither tape and just enjoyed the music, so thankful I wasn't down there on the freeway but was way up high instead, watching from my secluded vantage point.

The first of the month is a day to replenish and to renew. We all need to take time to refill our tanks in whatever way works for us. After all . . .

YOU CAN'T GIVE ANYTHING
IF YOUR OWN TANK IS EMPTY.

To refill my tank, I even make a celebration out of changing the sheets. There is nothing as fragrant and fun as fresh, clean sheets, don't you think?

Praise the Lord! It's Friday!

Making the first of the month a special day is just one example of how you can put more zest into your life, something that psychologists highly recommend. One mom with two grown children living lifestyles totally against their Christian upbringing wrote to share how she came to make Friday her special day:

> At one of my lowest times, bright and early one Friday morning as I prayed, I told God that *I* needed to be ministered to, that this was going to be *my* day, that for that one day I knew I could trust Him to take over these children we both loved. *Yes,* I thought, *I know I can do it for this one day.* God truly ministered to me that day. Any time the worry thoughts would try to creep in, I would say, "Thank You, God, for taking care of their needs today!" How God truly ministered to me that day!
>
> Then I decided that would be a great idea each week— to set aside Friday for God to minister to MY needs. A lot of the problems I worried about then have been resolved. It was the beginning of the return of joy into my life.
>
> Friday is still God's day to minister to ME. I look forward to it. I turn over anything I'm concerned about to God—for at least that one day. I dress as attractively as I can, put on my favorite perfume, and do everything that I feel God leading me to do. I praise Him and thank Him all day long, and I am strengthened in a marvelous way.
>
> I believe if parents who are hurting could let God take over for just one day, they would begin to have joy in their lives again. If my experience could help one person, I'm glad to share it.

Why Not a "Holiday" for Lost Loved Ones?

Not long ago I got another letter from a Spatula friend who had noticed that "Tim's holiday" was coming up. Then her letter went on to explain:

> In my support groups here and when I go to speak, I share with everyone the idea a bereaved father had in a letter to Compassionate Friends. He said we had a holiday for Washington, Lincoln, Martin Luther King, etc. Everyone important had a holiday. Well, the most important person

to him was his Kathy and he decided if no one else wanted to, *he* at least wanted her acknowledged during the year. So he chose the day of her death as Kathy's holiday.

He remarked he would take the day off work if it wasn't a weekend and each year he'd first go to the cemetery, telling Kathy about the happenings in the family. Then he'd spend the rest of the day doing something he knew she'd approve of, like visiting a museum, taking a day trip, a drive to the beach, whatever. He finished by saying, "In my heart of hearts I cannot let twelve months of the year go by without having my Kathy's holiday."

All of us who have lost a special treasure and hear of this idea think it's pretty neat. Didn't he say it well? And it's much easier to have that day approaching and thinking of it as a tribute day to our person than a day for just dreaded and frightful memories!

Anyway, your Tim sounded like such a terrific young man and a love to be around. He had great goals, enjoyed life, etc. How impossible to believe he could be wiped out after just talking to him! But how proud he is now of you two and your ministry!!

My Greg's "holiday" was one decade old last year, and so eleven years is coming up soon. I was just stunned that ten whole years had gone by. How I still wanted people to mention his name and remember he existed . . . you, too, I'm sure!

The first time I read this letter, I thought, *What a great way to change the anniversary of a death to a GOOD DAY.* Since then, I have celebrated Tim's holiday and Steven's holiday too.

It is said that the secret to joyful living is celebrating SOMETHING every day, no matter how insignificant it might seem. Maybe your schedule doesn't allow you to take a whole day for yourself, but you should spend at least a few minutes on a special activity you enjoy.

How to Receive "Guaranteed" Gifts

One way to put more celebration into your life is to start by at least being sure you'll have your own present for each of the special holidays, which are always important to women. I talk to many gals who go through most of the holidays without receiving a nice giftwrapped present with their own name on it. Oh, yes, they wrap presents for others, but somehow their husbands give one gift—usually at Christmas—that is supposed to last for the whole year. Other important days like birthdays, Mother's Day, anniversaries, and Valentine's Day may go unnoticed.

There is a FABULOUS REMEDY for this problem. Here's what you can do. Right after the first of the year (when most stores have sales and mark things way down) find a store that sells nice little gifts and does courtesy giftwrapping as well. Pick out at least five presents for yourself to cover your birthday, Valentine's Day, Mother's Day, wedding anniversary, and Christmas. They needn't be costly. Something for around five dollars is usually enough to qualify for free giftwrapping.

I buy my special gifts at nearby Knott's Berry Farm, where they do lovely giftwrapping. Then I bring my five presents home and place them around the house in prominent spots where I'll have to move them as I clean. That way they get shifted around so much I forget what is in which package, then each one is a surprise when I open it.

This idea works beautifully. When anyone asks you what your husband gave you for your birthday or for Mother's Day, you can proudly show them the lovely gift that you "received." (Be discreet. They don't have to know you bought it for yourself.)

Your husband should be delighted. In fact, you will both wind up happy as clams because he is relieved of shopping, which most men hate to do, and you have something you wanted. Not only that, but your beautifully wrapped gifts will decorate your home much of the year, and you can enjoy the sparkly paper and shiny ribbon as you anticipate opening each package.

This idea works so well you may want to extend it into buying little gifts you can open on the first of each month. I'm considering doing that because when I only buy five gifts, by the time Valentine's Day comes around, I've already shared mine and they're ALL GONE!

One friend dropped by last year just after I had purchased my five presents and had placed them around the house. She was in desperate straits with a real need to feel special. So, there went one gift to her. Then another friend came over who had just learned she had a suspicious lump in her breast. I knew she would enjoy a special gift, and there went a second one.

A few days later, some friends dropped by and I learned their son was dying of AIDS. Naturally, they couldn't go away without a special little remembrance.

Then there was a visit from a friend whose son was killed in a plane crash. How comforting it was, after we prayed together, to place in her hands another of the gifts I had bought for myself.

So it wasn't even Valentine's Day yet, and already four of my gifts were gone! During the first week of February, we were surprised by a visit from an old college friend who happened to be in the area. How wonderful it was to renew old memories together. And when I learned it was her birthday, I couldn't let her go without a gift.

So now all five of my special gifts were gone, but what a multiple blessing they had all been to me. First, I had enjoyed buying the gifts for myself (selfish as that may seem). Second, I had enjoyed looking at the beautifully wrapped packages as they decorated our living room. And then, when I had shared my gifts and watched my friends open them, it was a triple blessing to see their delight.

Because I may give my gifts away, I make sure the wrapping paper is not indicative of any special holiday. I just ask the giftwrap department to make it shiny and fun—a celebration kind of paper. This way, I can share any of the gifts whenever I want.

I've been celebrating with gifts I've bought for myself for the past couple of years, but I find that they never last until my birthday in December or until Christmas. But what fun I have had in sharing them! Each person who received one of my gifts thought it was purchased expressly for her. It doesn't matter that I really bought them for myself. Once I see a need, I'm happy to share because of the boomerang effect that brings so much pleasure back to me. And besides, if I give away all my gifts before it's time to open them, I just start all over again, going back down to the gift shop to replace them with new ones!

As we celebrate with others, we ourselves enjoy celebrating.

"Suzy's Zoo" illustration © '92 Suzy Spafford. Used by permission.

Merrymaking on a Budget

If your budget won't allow any gift buying right now, it doesn't matter. Celebrations don't have to be expensive. If you look around, you can find dozens of small ways to celebrate that are not costly, fattening, or illegal. One of the best definitions of celebration I've seen is "merrymaking," and there are unlimited ways to do that.

For example, have you ever been driving on the freeway, sailing along just beautifully and then look over at the opposing traffic to notice that it is stalled for miles and miles. When that happens, I get a sudden JOY and am so thankful I'm going the opposite way!

Or have you ever stained a dress, washed it, and then have all the stain COME OUT? That IS something special, and so is having all the socks come out of the dryer in even pairs. And what about balancing your checkbook so it actually comes out right or is only a few dollars off? For me, THAT is fabulous, and I celebrate!

When we buy groceries, Bill and I each try to guess how much the total amount will be before we get to the checkout stand. The one who is closest to the correct total gets a special prize. I am sure the cashier and bag boy must see us coming up to the checkout stand, and they probably joke about the couple who competes for a prize by making the best GUESSTIMATE on their grocery total. At least it provides a little change from their routine because they finally have customers who actually ENJOY getting their cash register receipt. Bill usually wins, so he rewards himself with an ice cream cone or other treat.

Actually, you don't have to let one day go by without finding SOMETHING to celebrate—even something that others might think is insignificant. Have you ever celebrated having some flowers finally bloom in your backyard? How about celebrating when you finish a sweater you've been knitting for the last six months?

Celebration Ideas Are Practically Limitless

The things you can do to celebrate are unlimited. Here are three more relatively inexpensive ideas you may want to adapt, or they may trigger your own ideas that are better:

- Call up a friend and invite her over to bake cookies or make candy with you. Then giftwrap what you make and take it to someone who would really appreciate it. Have your children help, and when they ask you what the special occasion is, just say, "No special occasion—we just want to celebrate by doing something nice for someone else."

- You can turn weekends into special occasions with a celebration breakfast—on a Saturday perhaps. (If you attend church, Sunday mornings are usually a bit too hectic.) The menu for your celebration breakfast should be the

specialties your family likes. Or you may want to invite friends over for waffles, pancakes, or those special omelets that only you can make. Be sure to have a nice selection of your favorite jellies and jams, something with your special touch on it. The idea is not to spend your weekend trying to finish all those "to-do" lists that didn't get done throughout the week. I've always liked this little quip about how hectic life can get:

THINGS TO
— DO TODAY —

Find the list!

But on Saturdays, forget all that hassle—in fact, LOSE THE LIST and just celebrate Saturday as a day off from your regular workweek—a day when you can "do as you please." Keep it free of daily chores.

• If you have a fireplace, select a rainy day and invite a friend over for tea, or make it for lunch, if you like. Put a pretty cloth over the coffee table in front of the fire, or just use a card table. Remember, you don't need a "special occasion." Just celebrating your friendship together is

enough. Of course, one of you may have just received an encouraging letter from a child in college or perhaps from a grown child who is married and living far away. There are dozens of reasons to celebrate, if you only look for them![1]

Life Is Short—Celebrate Now!

One of the reasons we should celebrate more is that life goes by faster than we can imagine. Before we know it, we've missed out on enjoying so many wonderful things because we feel we should save them for "Sunday-best." Or perhaps we wait for that special occasion that never seems to arrive.

Like me, you may have read more than one report of how someone dies and the surviving relatives find all kinds of beautiful things that were never used. Furniture in a front parlor may never have been sat upon. New baby clothes might be forgotten in a drawer because they were too nice for a baby to spit up on, and of course, the baby outgrew them. Beautifully embroidered towels may be hidden in another drawer, obviously saved for that special occasion that never seemed to come.

It may be this way throughout the house. The dear person who passed on had saved all her beautiful things for special occasions that never came.

Whenever I read or hear stories like this, it reminds me that it's easy to deny yourself many of life's simple pleasures simply because you want to be "practical." That's why I'm such an advocate of having a JOY BOX, which, in my case, has grown into a JOY ROOM, twelve feet wide and sixty feet long.

For years I've urged folks to become "joy collectors." It doesn't cost much, if anything, to start. All you need is a shoe box decorated with bright, shiny paper. Over the years, hundreds, if not thousands, of Spatula gals have started their own Joy Boxes filled with simple little things—cartoons, poems, and quips or quotes cut out of the *Love Line* newsletter or from newspapers or magazines.

Special cards received for Mother's Day, birthdays, etc., are also naturals for your Joy Box. Your Joy Box collection doesn't

"Suzy's Zoo" illustration © '82 Suzy Spafford. Used by permission.

have to be expensive. The only requirement is that everything in your box be a SPIRIT-LIFTER—something that encourages you and makes you smile. For example, a friend just sent me this:

A HUG DELIGHTS AND WARMS AND CHARMS,
IT MUST BE WHY GOD GAVE US ARMS.

Back when we started Spatula, I used to go out and buy inexpensive thongs at Thrifty Drug Stores, just so I could have enough empty shoe boxes to decorate for folks who came to our meetings. Eventually, I had so many pairs of thongs around I decided there must be a cheaper way to help folks start their own Joy Boxes. So I began using empty envelope boxes left after we mail out our *Love Line* newsletter. We always have plenty of them around, and they make great Joy Boxes.

Our Quillows Bring Us Lots of Joy

Since starting Spatula I've received literally hundreds of fun things from folks who wanted to share their joy with me. Recently a darling gal named Bertie sent Bill and me our own personal QUILLOWS. In her note she explained that some people call them "magic pillows" because they look like PILLOWS, but they open to become QUILTS that you can take on picnics or use to cover your feet while watching TV.

As you might guess, my quillow is covered with geraniums. Bill's has a cute little teddy bear on it. Bill is good at bear hugs, so I think the teddy bear on his quillow is a perfect symbol of his caring heart.

Bertie has made more than three hundred quillows over the past few years and is still at it—sharing her joy in this novel way. Every time Bill and I snuggle down under our quillows, I think about how God never gives us a "guilt quilt." Instead, His comfort blanket is always warm and snugly, like the quillows Bertie made for us.

Why Not Become a Joy Collector?

Spatulanders keep sending me new additions to my Joy Room almost every week. I especially like the big, bright colorful banner with letters in green, red, blue, and yellow that says, "LET'S CELEBRATE!" Another recent arrival is a phone shaped like a train. When the phone rings, the train goes *CLANG-CLANG . . . CHOO-CHOO . . .* and whistles, so it's fun to have folks call and hear my telephone train chug away.

Since writing *Geranium*, I have received every conceivable kind of geranium joy item. I have geranium hats, plates, potholders, and towels. I even have a pair of slippers with geraniums stitched on them as well as a stained-glass yellow sunbonnet with a red geranium adorning it.

Everything in my Joy Room delights me because so much of it reflects the love out there that has come back to Bill and me. Sometimes I think we should call it our Boomerang Room, because the love we have sent out through books and newsletters has ministered to many folks who now want to send back to us some of the joy that has been infused into their hearts. To paraphrase the familiar saying, "What goes around comes around, SOMETIMES TENFOLD."

When you develop the habit of being a joy collector, you have your own built-in therapy. Joy is everywhere. All you have to do is look for it and then use it instead of saving it for Sunday-best or a special occasion.

Having a Joy Box, or even a Joy Room, is one of the best ways to stay in a frame of mind that celebrates life instead of letting it go by with the simple pleasures unused. As one lady said in her brief note to me, "I listened to your tape yesterday and today—what a blessing! Even though we have never met, I feel close to you because of your honesty. You've taught me to fill my surroundings with joy—so now I don't buy anything unless it's 'happy.' It really helps!"

Try Giving Gifts without Ribbons

There are lots of neat things we can share with others. It's like throwing pebbles in a pond and watching the ripples go out, SCATTERING JOY. Scattering gifts of joy doesn't have to be expensive. There is great joy in the small things in life. Don't wait until you can give someone a gift that is "worthy" or "significant." Any small gift will do if your heart is big enough, because:

THE BEST GIFTS ARE TIED
WITH HEART STRINGS—YOURS.

And remember that perhaps some of the best gifts have no ribbons or wrappings at all. Friends give each other gifts without ribbons every time they get together, simply by exchanging kindness and love.

A Spatula friend wrote to tell me of a "special gift" she gave to her elderly mom by reading *Geranium* to her ALOUD. She explained:

> At that time she was blind because of radiation therapy to the brain; she had no hair and was very weak due to the cancer in her body. But you know what? We both laughed and enjoyed ourselves immensely while reading this book together. Just one and a half years before that, my mom had lost a son (my brother) due to a drunk driver. She was uplifted by your book. She went to meet my brother and her Lord last spring.
>
> The two of us absorbing your book is a wonderful memory for me. She was like you in a lot of ways. She was a godly woman who loved to laugh and play jokes. She always chose to be a positive, optimistic person and not let her pain destroy her life. Even when diagnosed with cancer, she considered it a privilege to suffer, and displayed Christ in her sufferings.

This mother and daughter gave each other "a gift without ribbons." And of all the gifts that are given, often it is the gifts without ribbons that are appreciated the most. So listen, encourage, praise, share time, show concerns, smile, and remember:

LIFE IS WONDERFUL . . .
DO YOUR BEST NOT TO MISS IT!

Bugaboo Busters

SMILE . . . IT MAY NOT MAKE YOU FEEL BETTER
BUT IT'S SURE TO MAKE SOMEONE ELSE FEEL BETTER.

Some people are too tired to give you a smile. Give them one of yours, as no one needs a smile so much as he who has no more to give.

Be more cheerful . . . more.

LIVE EACH DAY AS IF IT WERE YOUR LAST.
SOMEDAY YOU'LL BE RIGHT.

Whenever you're down and out . .
lift up your head and . . .
SMILE!

CONSIDERING THE CIRCUMSTANCES . . . SMILE.
ENJOY WHAT IS . . . BEFORE IT ISN'T.

Six Realities We Cannot Change

1. Everyone grows older. "So teach us to number our days, that we may apply our hearts unto wisdom" (Ps. 90:12).

2. Life is tough and hard, a constant struggle. "Man that is born of a woman is . . . full of trouble" (Job. 14:1).

3. Life is not always fair. "Of those eighteen, upon whom the tower in Siloam fell, and slew them, think ye that they were sinners above all men that dwell in Jerusalem?" (Luke 13:4).

4. No matter how winsome we are, we can't make everyone like us. Even of Jesus it was said, "Can there any good come out of Nazareth?" (John 1:46). "And they laughed Him to scorn" (Mark 5:40).

5. No matter how hard we try, we can't change anyone. "O, Jerusalem . . . how often would I have gathered thy children together, . . . and ye would not!" (Luke 13:34). Each person, with God's help and our encouragement, must decide to change.

6. No matter how dark the outlook, we can't change the fact (or wouldn't want to!) that God scatters serendipities (surprise blessings) in our path. "Weeping may endure for a night, but joy cometh in the morning" (Ps. 30:5b).

Reprinted by permission from Robert J. Hastings, author of *The Station and Other Gems of Joy*. All Scripture verses are KJV.

EACH DAY COMES
BEARING ITS GIFTS.
UNTIE THE RIBBONS!

There are two approaches to the future: anxiety and optimism. One will make you dread tomorrow; the other will help you welcome it.

The important thing for us as Christians is not what we eat or drink but stirring up goodness and peace and joy from the Holy Spirit. (Rom. 14:17 TLB)

8

Year-Long Resolutions: Hope for the Best, Be Prepared for the Worst, and Take What Comes with a Smile

*I*f you're like me, the new year brings ambivalent feelings. The bad news is that the year starts with January, which, for many, is a dark, bleak, rainy, snowy, frozen month that consists of thirty-one Mondays in a row.

An ironic thing about the new year is that it makes us look back on the old year and think of how we messed up in one way or another. The good news, however, is that January brings a FRESH NEW START. January is a reminder that God designed things so that we get 365 fresh new starts every year, with twelve "first-of-the-months" thrown in for good measure.

What happens when you break one of your New Year's resolutions? What seems to work for me is to turn it into a year-long resolution or goal and reset it again, usually around the first of every month. We all have our own ideas on what kinds of resolutions to set, but here are some favorites that I make my goals all year long:

1. Avoid Grumbling, Particularly Out Loud

Grumbling and other ill-natured remarks are guaranteed to create friction with your family or your friends. We all have our days, however, when we're tempted to grumble because we can't see good in the world anywhere.

Recently my friend, Lynda, and I were zipping along a crowded freeway, headed for a church luncheon where I was scheduled to speak. Suddenly we heard a roaring sound. Lynda thought it was a train passing by, but then we heard an EXPLOSION and I knew it was no train. The bumping told me it was my right rear tire.

Somehow, other cars behind us saw our plight and let us struggle from the fast lane all the way over to the right shoulder, where we just managed to park on a narrow strip next to a concrete wall. We were so close to the wall Lynda couldn't even get out of her door on the passenger side. With the cars whizzing by on my driver's side, I didn't dare try to get out my door either.

As we sat there frantically wondering how we would EVER be rescued, Lynda took out a sheet of paper and scrawled HELP on it in big letters. She is proportioned much like I am—neither one of us is in the "petite" category—but somehow she managed to crawl over the seat and put her makeshift sign in the back window. Then she had to crawl BACK over the seat again, and we just sat there hoping that someone speeding by could read her sign.

After what seemed like an eternity, a policeman on a motorcycle stopped and said he would send help. Off he went looking for a tow truck, but we never did see him again—or a tow truck. Finally, a small white pickup with an Ohio license plate miraculously appeared and parked directly behind us. The driver was a young man in his twenties; evidently he was new to California and didn't realize how dangerous our freeways can be. I was so grateful to him for stopping I would have kissed him, but I couldn't get out of the car. Instead, I pressed the button that opened the trunk so he could get to the spare tire.

Because I was on the way to speak, the trunk was loaded with boxes of books, tapes, and props I use when speaking. So the poor kid had to unload ALL that stuff and stack it on the side of the freeway so he could get to the little spare tire. He finally got to the tire, found the jack and other tools, and knelt down to change the blown-out tire. The cars were whizzing by and the wind was blowing like crazy. In a minute he yelled to me, "I need the little KEY to unlock the hubcap so I can get the tire off!"

"Key?" I yelled back. "WHAT KEY?" I decided he meant the car keys, so I tossed them back to where he was kneeling.

"No," he said as he tossed them back. "You must have a little key somewhere to unlock the wire-wheel hubcap. Then I can get your tire off."

I'd never heard of such a thing. For that matter, I'd never had a flat before. Bill always took care of things like this. What key could he be talking about? In desperation, I yelled to him to pry the hubcap off or break off the bolts or whatever he had to do— because I didn't understand what KEY he was talking about.

"Are you sure you want me to pry it off?" he yelled back. "It will ruin the hubcap, and maybe the tire rim too."

"Who cares?" I shouted. "We will all die out here, so do what you have to do—I don't care what it costs—just GET THE DUMB HUBCAP OFF!"

So, without grumbling once, our good Samaritan banged, twisted, and pried. Finally, after ruining the hubcap completely, he managed to loosen the lug nuts, take off the blown tire, and put on the little spare. Then he had to pack all the books, tapes, and other stuff back into the trunk. It took quite awhile, but he worked steadily, smiling and shaking his head now and then. But he never complained.

As he was finishing up, I asked Lynda to look in the glove compartment to find a notepad so we could get his address and send him some money for all his help. As Lynda rummaged around, she came upon a little manila envelope. Printed on the outside in big black letters was: THIS IS YOUR LOCK PROOF HUBCAP KEY.

We opened up the envelope and took out the key, but it was more like a *tool*, not a key. By this time the young man had finished and he inched up to my window (with cars zooming by less than three feet away) to tell me he would help me get into the traffic lane so we wouldn't get plowed into by another car.

As he turned to go back to his truck, I victoriously held up the "key" he had been asking for. He saw it, and I was sure that now he would at least make a face, but he just smiled and waved, then hopped into his truck.

Somehow he pulled out into the lane of traffic and signaled the other cars to go around, and that allowed us to get back onto the freeway without getting hit. And to top it off, he followed us all the way to our turnoff. We were late for the luncheon, but our adventure gave me some fresh material for talking about how to deal with stress!

Later, on the way home, I began wondering what I would tell Bill. Should I just toss the envelope, key and all, under the front seat and let on that I couldn't FIND IT? Should I go someplace and buy another hubcap before I got home rather than tell him what happened? Or should I be really dramatic when telling him about it and make him feel grateful that I got home ALIVE, even at the cost of a ruined hubcap?

I decided it was best to simply tell Bill the truth. When I finished, I waited for him to bawl me out and complain about how much wire-wheel hubcaps cost. Amazingly, he wasn't upset with me. In fact, he was calm and almost apologetic because he hadn't explained to me about the little "key/tool thing."

In fact, Bill actually took ALL the blame for my not knowing what the key was or where it was kept. I began wondering how lucky I could get. First, the driver of the pickup had gone to all that trouble to help us and never grumbled once, and now Bill was being a doll about it too! (I appreciated Bill's non-grumbling attitude so much. After all, to a woman, a key is a key, not some odd-shaped tool that's *called* a key but doesn't even resemble one!)

Later, Bill went to the car dealer and ordered a new wire-wheel hubcap, at a cost of eighty-five dollars, but he never complained about THAT either. I appreciated that too. In fact, his whole response to my hubcap adventure inspired me to write my own paraphrase of the well-known Serenity Prayer:

God grant me (not my spouse, my kids, or even good friends like Lynda, although they all may need it too)

the Serenity (that is, the capacity to be tranquil, unruffled, unflappable in spite of it ALL)
to Accept (not just endure, suffer, or bear)
the Things (as well as the PEOPLE in my life)
I cannot Change (even though I've tried and tried),
the Courage (which can only come from You, Lord)
to Change the Things I Can (particularly about myself—and You and I know there's plenty to work on!)
and the Wisdom (perceptiveness, foresight, discernment, and sound judgment)
to Know (not just "guess" or "hope")
the Difference (when I'm in Your will and when I simply want my own).[1]

2. Laugh . . . Out Loud . . . and Often

One of my favorite sources of fun is a little magazine called *Laughing Matters* edited by Joel Goodman, who also gives workshops on the power of humor. He says, "Humor is power. You can't often control situations around you, but you can control your internal responses to them with humor. That's power."[2]

Goodman believes that humor is serious business, and I certainly agree. That's why it's good to resolve at least once a month that you'll laugh—a lot. We'll all live longer if we can loosen up and enjoy life.

I love the letter that came from one lady who had been in her own deadly pit of problems and was trying to figure out how she'd go forward with the rest of her life. She told me her friends see her as battered but stronger because of all her experiences, but inside she doesn't feel all that strong—more like a "mush melon living in a middle-aged frame."

This mom loves to get the *Love Line* because, as she put it, "My heart sees you sort of like a plumber with the 'unclog' for the cesspool and a plate of chocolate-chip cookies for the sinking heart. Thank you! Thank God for your reminding me we may as well laugh and roll or we will cry, dry out completely, and snap. Our Father does, indeed, have a sense of humor. Guess He simply has to . . ."

This lady is right. As somebody said,

LIFE IS FAR TOO SERIOUS
TO MANAGE WITHOUT HUMOR.[3]

As you resolve to laugh more this year, just keep in mind that every day will bring lots of reasons to chuckle. If you don't find your own, here are some tongue-in-cheek observations to give you a jump-start:

- At least five times each day, someone in an aerobics class turns up lame.
- Dentists get plaque and cavities too.
- Really rich people are much more likely to die racing at Monte Carlo.
- IRS employees have to pay taxes too.

Try the Bunny-Slipper Approach

As we noted in an earlier chapter, it's healthy to be willing to laugh at yourself and make light of your shortcomings. We all have our quirks, so we shouldn't take ourselves too seriously. One of the best solutions I know for that is to take the "bunny-slipper approach," a philosophy of life we all need to practice.

A friend sent me a pair of bunny slippers, and every now and then I put them on, especially when I'm tempted to start thinking I'm important or "nearly famous." There's something about bunny slippers that keeps my perspective where it belongs, but in addition to that, my bunny slippers remind me that whatever happens doesn't have to get me down. I can still be a little silly and laugh and enjoy life. Pain dissolves, frustrations vanish, and burdens roll away when I have on my bunny slippers.

Have you ever thought much about God's sense of humor? In the following quote, an unknown author ponders whether

God could ever take us as seriously as we take ourselves. He (or she) wrote, "God's humor is not mocking; it does not condescend. It does not dash across our skies like lightning but bubbles up from the mulch on the floor of our daily life. God laughs because He knows more than we do. God has sharper vision."

Doesn't He, though? One of my favorite poems is "The Land of Beginning Again," by Louisa Fletcher. One of her stanzas sums up my motivation to make laughter a year-long resolution:

> For what had been hardest we'd know had been best,
>   And what had seemed loss would be gain;
> For there isn't a sting that will not take wing
>   When we've faced it and laughed it away;
> And I think that the laughter is most what we're after
>   In the Land of Beginning Again.[4]

3. Always Greet Folks with a Smile

Remember that a lot of your friends (not to mention strangers) are carrying frowns in their own hearts. A smile can literally make their day.

Not long ago I arrived just after dinner at a conference grounds where I would speak the next morning. I wanted to hear the evening speaker, but because she had already started I had to CRAWL over three or four ladies to get to one seat that was in the back row of the crowded lecture room. Because it was hot, each lady was sipping a glass of water, and as I tried to get past one gal, I inadvertently bumped her arm, spilling her water all over her lap!

I apologized profusely as she fussed and fumed, dabbing at her lap with a tissue while making loud remarks about rude people coming late. It was obvious she was VERY upset with me for spilling water on her, and of course, I was mortified. Several gals had seen what had happened and several more heard her talking loudly about how careless I had been.

The next day, I was the keynote speaker for the morning session. Later, as I was signing autographs, a kind lady who had been sitting next to the woman on whom I had spilled water, whispered in my ear, "This morning, when she learned who you were, she began saying, 'BARBARA JOHNSON SPILLED WATER ON ME.'"

I looked down the line, and there SHE was, waiting her turn to get her book autographed. As I signed several more books, I wondered what I would write in her book. *(Maybe it would be better not to write ANYTHING.)* As her turn came, I just asked her name and then underneath I wrote, "BAPTIZED BY BARB." Then I handed it back to her with a big smile. She looked at what I had written and for a second I wasn't sure how she'd react. But, much to my relief, she laughed really hard. When I tried to apologize again she graciously said, "Oh, it was nothing."

A smile can go a long way toward smoothing out awkward situations. So always have one ready for everyone. You say you don't have a whole lot to smile about? That may be true, especially if life has dealt you a nasty blow. One mom, however, wrote the following little note, which makes my heart smile:

> Just a note to let you know how much I appreciate you and your monthly newsletter. It's about the only thing I look forward to since my son's death. Some days I feel I'll never smile or be happy again, then I'll pick up one of your letters and catch myself smiling. Thanks so much.

If you start thinking about it, there are lots of things that could happen this year that might make you smile. Here are twelve possible smile-makers—one for each month. They may not really happen, but just thinking about these serendipities may cheer you up:

1. Your son comes home from college and does his own laundry.

2. Your fifteen-year-old son wanders into the kitchen and asks, "What can I do to help?"

3. Your husband remembers your birthday AND your anniversary, all in one year!

4. Your kids (or grandkids) go to bed the first time they are asked.

5. Your boss says, "You've really been putting in long hours. Take the afternoon off with pay."

6. Your mother-in-law comes for dinner and your husband doesn't remind you of what a great cook she is.

7. Your twenty-seven-year-old son comes down for breakfast and says, "Mom, I've got a job and I'm moving out on Friday."

8. Your teenager returns your car, washed, vacuumed, and full of gas!

9. Your doctor takes your blood pressure and his eyes don't get as big as saucers.

10. Your husband turns off the TV, serves you a cup of coffee, and says, "What would you like to talk about?"

11. You try on the dress you bought after getting over the five-day flu and it still fits three months later.

12. Your auto mechanic says, "There's no charge—all you had was a loose wire."

4. Be an Encourager

If you're going to encourage other folks, the best place to start is with yourself. Collect only "life-lifters" and discard all the "life-sinkers."

> ENJOY THE LITTLE THINGS.
> ONE DAY YOU MAY LOOK BACK AND REALIZE . . .
> THEY WERE THE BIG THINGS.

If you look hard enough, you can see the positive and even humorous side of anything. One lady who faced surgery for breast cancer found a creative way to do that. When the orderlies came to wheel her into the operating room, they found her wearing a propeller beanie on her head and a large colorful sign

Lift your life with laughter!

"Suzy's Zoo" illustration © '93 Suzy Spafford. Used by permission.

on her chest. The sign said, "GIVE IT YOUR BEST SHOT!" A smaller note attached to the sign said, "Do not remove this sign until the surgeon sees it."

In the operating room, one of the nurses saw the sign and the note and asked her what it meant. She smiled and replied, "Well, when that surgeon cuts on me today, I just want him to be in a REAL GOOD MOOD!"

With a positive attitude, tears of sorrow will start to glisten with gladness. In fact, tears bring the rainbows into our lives, and at the end of those rainbows we can find colorful pots of joy if we only LOOK. One Spatulander wrote a lovely little rainbow note that said:

> I read in a book a couple of years ago a statement about encouragement that I don't think I'll ever forget:
>
> ONE WORD OR NOTE BRINGS MORE
> ENCOURAGEMENT
> THAN A THOUSAND THOUGHTS . . .
> NEVER EXPRESSED.
>
> So here's your little "note of encouragement" from me to encourage you in your outreach to others. You're a very real and authentic ambassador for our Lord. People identify with genuine people . . . and the sense of humor God has given you is very REFRESHING. KEEP UP THE GOOD WORK . . . as unto Him.

The word *encourage* means "to fill the heart," and these words gave me just what I needed that day. All of us need encouragement—the gentle touch that helps us "lighten up." Make it a constant habit to ENCOURAGE YOURSELF by being a joy collector. By the end of the year, the joy room of your heart will be overflowing!

There are many ways to collect joy. Here are just a few that have worked for me:

> If you want joy for half an hour, take a bubble bath.
> If you want joy for an afternoon, go shopping.
> If you want joy for an evening, go out to dinner.
> If you want joy for a day, kidnap your husband and go on a picnic.
> If you want joy for a week, go on vacation (or send the kids to camp).
> If you want joy for a month, spend within your budget.
> If you want joy for life, invest time in others.

Karl Menninger, the famous psychiatrist, was answering questions from the audience after giving a lecture, and one man

asked, "What would you advise a person to do if he felt a nervous breakdown coming on?"

Most of those present expected Menninger to reply, "Consult
a psychiatrist," but to their astonishment he said, "Lock up
your house and go across the railroad tracks to find someone in
need. Then do something to help that person." That could just
be the best advice Menninger ever gave anyone, but it was
hardly new and original. Remember what King Solomon said
thousands of years ago:

AS WE REFRESH OTHERS,
WE OURSELVES ARE REFRESHED.[5]

When you share joy and encouragement, it comes back to you
many-fold. For proof, I have many letters like the following:

> Praise the Lord! Thanks for your joy and encouragement!
> We have just finished passing around your book at work—
> *what fun!* It's time to get another, so we can start the EN-
> COURAGEMENT CYCLE once again.

- - - - - - -

> I know you understand how we get locked up in our per-
> sonal trials sometimes and can't always function at our
> best. I used to be able to handle a million things at a time,
> now I am regaining composure after a "trip through the
> pits." I know you say "Amen!" You have been there and
> understand. God bless you for caring about the rest of us.

- - - - - - -

> Your book helps me retain the proper perspective; there
> is still laughter and love all about us! How lucky I, person-
> ally, am—and you helped me grasp that. I can't thank you
> enough. God bless!

These letters are treasures, because they tell me Spatula is
making a difference. As somebody said:

LOVE CURES PEOPLE—BOTH THE ONES WHO GIVE IT
AND THE ONES WHO RECEIVE IT.

5. Be Thankful—Especially for Your Family

One of the best builders of a positive attitude is to be aware continually of how God blesses us each day. As somebody said:

FOR EVERY ONE THING THAT GOES WRONG
THERE ARE FIFTY TO ONE HUNDRED BLESSINGS.
COUNT THEM!

Of course, all of us who have been privileged to be mothers know that things can go wrong now and then. One mom wrote:

> I am hurting so bad by the mistakes and problems of our wayward son. He just does not learn from his mistakes, and the older he gets the bigger the mistakes get. So many emotions involved—love, anger, wanting to help, shame, disappointment, and hurts—it's a roller-coaster ride and I wish it would stop. He wants circumstances to change so he won't have to!

Another mom told about her son, who is addicted to drugs. He lives in their city, but not their home. On the day this mom wrote to me, it was a good day because at least she wasn't in the middle of some crisis with her son. As of the day before they knew where he was and she knew he had a job. In fact, he had kept this job for almost a week—a record. And then she put the AMBIVALENCE a lot of parents feel so beautifully:

> I have read your books and enjoyed them so much. I sit with tears running down my cheeks, laughing so hard my sides hurt. But I guess that's what it is all about:
>
> MOTHERHOOD:
> BOUNDLESS JOY SURROUNDED
> BY BOTTOMLESS PITS.

Being a parent is a long-term investment, not a short-term note. Someone said that becoming a parent is like getting a life sentence in prison with no hope of parole. Any way you look at it, parenting is a long haul, and there is no way to resign! Learn all the ways of doing it the best you can, then trust the results to God.

Of course, just when you're sure your kids have forgotten you, one of them will do something nice. For Bill's birthday last year, our youngest son, Barney, gave him a huge GOLD-PLATED tape measure. It was inscribed:

I CAN'T MEASURE WHAT YOU'VE MEANT IN MY LIFE.

Bill treasures that tape measure above all else and proudly displays it on his desk. A part of the inscription also says, "To B.J. from B.J." I like to tease Bill about that—after all, my initials are B.J. too!

A Family Is for Appreciating

The experiences of the last twenty-seven years, beginning with Bill's crippling accident in 1966, have all served to make me increasingly appreciative of how priceless a family really is. Yes, families have their tense times, but being in a family constantly reminds us:

THE BEST THINGS IN LIFE AREN'T THINGS.

Appreciation is a kindling force. When we truly appreciate folks, we see them in a completely new light. Whole libraries have been written about the family, but I think the entire subject can be put into one statement:

THE ONLY WAY TO LIVE HAPPILY WITH FOLKS
IS TO OVERLOOK THEIR FAULTS AND ADMIRE
THEIR VIRTUES.

You can't change people, so why not enjoy the good parts? A clear definition of love could be: "practicing the art of appreciation." The poet Robert Browning said, "Take away love and this

Words of love can not compare ...
To the time you give for us to share !
Thank you for living life **with** me!

My beloved is mine and I am his... Song of Songs 2:16

© "Sonshine Promises" created by Gretchen Clasby, Cedar Hill Studio.
Used by permission.

earth is a tomb." The medical doctor William Menninger repeatedly said, "Love is the medicine for most of mankind's ills." It's also the medicine for most of our personal ills.

The neurotic wants and wants and wants love—but doesn't want to give it. The neurotic is afraid to try, afraid of being hurt. It's much easier to complain, be angry, and take from others. A mature person, however, is ready to give love whether or not it is returned. To be willing to give love, whether you get any back or not, is a strong mark of mental health. It's easy to love the lovable; it takes spiritual grace to love the unlovable. But when you give love freely, you usually DO get it back.

To those who know how to give love, marriage is life's greatest bargain. When spouses can be best friends, the bargain includes a bonus. After the children have flown the nest, parents are left with just each other. It can be a cozy, comfortable time of true affection, or it can turn into a period of indifference—living in the same house but not sharing together.

Love can be fresh for couples who learn how to give each other solid emotional support through the years. Marriage starts off with a treasure chest of gold—the love each partner feels for each other. The treasury must not become empty. Every act of devotion puts more love into the marital strong box. Every unloving act takes some out. When the treasure box is full, we live on a high note of secure confidence. Partners are able to make rich exchanges of sentiment. But when the treasury is empty, life is bankrupt with nothing but a dreary succession of empty days ahead.

They say love, like wine, improves with age. Wise spouses cherish each other more with each passing year. I enjoy the way Bill makes a fuss over me, and I still remember the day he came home with a fleecy lamb's-wool cover for the mattress. That was fine! A couple of days later, he brought home a fluffy goose-down comforter—terrific! About a week after that, he came home with two bed pillows made of soft duck feathers and announced proudly: "Now you have a LAMB to sleep on, a DUCK to lay your head on, and a GOOSE comforter to cover you, plus a BUFFALO BILL next to you!"

A Thankful Heart Is a Happy Heart

Being thankful is like an analogy I once read that talks of being given a dish of sand and being told there were particles of iron in it. We could look for the iron by sifting our clumsy fingers through the sand, but we wouldn't find much. If we took a magnet, however, and pulled it through the sand, it would draw to itself the almost invisible iron particles. The unthankful heart, like the clumsy fingers, discovers no mercies, but let the thankful heart sweep through the day, and as the magnet finds the iron, so will the thankful heart find heavenly blessings every time!

The twin sister of thankfulness is praise. One of my favorite verses is Isaiah 61:3, which speaks of "putting on the garment of praise for the spirit of heaviness." How I love that verse, especially since a darling gal out there in Spatula-land wrote the following poem for all to enjoy:

> A garment is mentioned in God's Word
> That fits every lady He made.
> It's lovely and beautiful, modish and chic
> And guaranteed never to fade.
> Its fit is perfect and never too long. . . .
> It's never too short and always in style . . .
> In fact, it's a garment you'll love!
> This garment is "PRAISE" with a heart full of joy,
> For then your heaviness goes.
> You'll feel a new peace and sorrow will cease
> And leave in your heart a new glow.
> With heaviness gone and your heart filled with song
> Sing praise to the Lord on His throne.
> He's dwelling inside and will comfort
> And guide each one who is truly His own.
> You're suitably dressed wearing garments of praise.
> The fit will be perfect on you.
> Just try it! You'll see! Then join in with me;
> Together we'll praise God anew!
>
> Norma Wiltse[6]

So, those are my five suggestions for year-long resolutions. You can add many others if you like. Come to think of it, there's a story going around that reminds me of one more very important resolve we all should make daily. It seems a woman in a red car pulled up to a tollbooth at the San Francisco-Oakland Bay Bridge. "I'm paying for myself and the six cars behind me," she said to the toll collector with a smile.

As the next six drivers pulled up to the booth, money in hand, the collector said, "Some lady up ahead paid your fare. Have a nice day!"

What motivated the woman to pay the toll for six perfect strangers? It turned out she had read a note taped on a friend's refrigerator:

PRACTICE RANDOM KINDNESS
AND SENSELESS ACTS OF BEAUTY.

Those words caught her imagination, and she decided to practice exactly what they said.[7] You may want to do the same. Don't worry about who it is or even why you're doing it. Kindness is not only contagious, it can multiply itself many-fold as those who receive a kind act are motivated to give one in turn. So start your own epidemic of kindness—in your family, your neighborhood, or where you work. And above all:

BE KIND TO UNKIND PEOPLE,
THEY PROBABLY NEED IT THE MOST!
Ashleigh Brilliant, Pot-shot
#406 © 1973

Bugaboo Busters

It is remarkable how the apostle Paul
covered so much territory and accomplished so much
without even a car.

LOVE IS NOT A MATTER OF COUNTING THE YEARS . . . IT'S MAKING THE YEARS COUNT.

If in the last year you haven't discarded a major opinion or acquired a new one, check your pulse. You may be dead!

You may not know all the answers, but you probably won't be asked all the questions, either.

You can learn many things from children. How much patience you have, for instance.[8]

You can no longer measure a home by inches, or weigh it by ounces, than you can set up the boundaries of a summer breeze or calculate the fragrance of a rose. Home is the love which is in it.[9]

IF MEN GOT PREGNANT . . . NATURAL CHILDBIRTH
WOULDN'T BE NEARLY AS POPULAR.

Children don't need critics as much as they need
role models, good examples, and plenty of "Nice going! You really did that well!"

SORROW LOOKS BACK . . .
WORRY LOOKS AROUND . . .
FAITH LOOKS UP.

If your eye is pure, there will be sunshine in your
soul. (Matt. 6:22 TLB)

Conclusion

Life Ain't No Ride on No Pink Duck, But So What?

*W*e have spent the last eight chapters looking at important ways to flatten out hurts and heartaches with humor as we build a positive attitude. But there is still one more tough question to deal with to make certain we aren't just trying to "escape reality":

How do we laugh and stay positive when God doesn't seem to care about our problems?

A mother with a homosexual child wrote to say she couldn't hold back the tears:

I can't talk about it without crying and I can't think about it without crying!!! You know, it's like we lost him in death—I just haven't buried him. The emotions and thoughts I have are just awful and the anger is starting. Yes, I pray daily. I beg for his reform, patience for me, and for guidance in interacting with him. . . .

Your book was great! I laughed and I cried and I felt all that you felt and thought. You know what? The pain is still dreadfully deep and I try to understand *why*. Why all this?

I feel very confident that our family will be healed. There are days that I start to wonder if it will happen, and these are times I find hard to deal with. I hate it when my faith starts to get thin. It scares me.

A wife who had been in the pit—"that dark disillusioning, lonely place"—wrote to tell about her dramatic conversion several years ago. She thought God would do the same for her adult children, who were immersed in many problems, from drug use to promiscuity, but it didn't happen. She felt the odds were overwhelming and admitted:

> I've always been the Christian who boldly witnessed. I unknowingly gave a lot of pat answers—three Scriptures and a prayer took care of everything. Now I speak little of Jesus' power to change situations because in mine He hasn't. . . . I've grown so weary. I've never been so without faith before. Floods of rage and anger flood from me— in swells. Six years of faithfulness to Him and I expected a reward *now*. My bubble about the God who can do *anything* has burst.

Another mom wrote about her adult children who had turned away from God to alcohol and drugs. While her church had joined her in praying for her children, things had only gotten worse—lost jobs, failures in college, and even attempted suicide. "This hurts so bad," she said. Then she added:

> Jesus is the only answer, but *when will He answer?* He answers prayers about everything else, even gave me a new paid-for car this summer. I'm home recuperating from extensive elbow surgery, and one of my church fellowship members gave me your book. I've cried through the first half of it and know you understand. Usually, I can find good or humor in most things, even when a hurricane took half my house and most of my trees. But this time it's my *babies*.

Adapted from Ashleigh Brilliant's Pot-shot #4852 © 1989.

Has Anyone Seen the Tunnel?

I get a lot of "when will Jesus answer?" letters. One said, "Why? God *could* do something if He wanted to. I don't understand. The only thing that I am sure of is that I wish I had never been born." Still another mom admitted, "The more I pray the less I hear or see any answers. Ever had that experience? I find prayer hard work—to keep on keeping on anyway!"

Yes, I HAVE had that experience. Prayer *is* hard work, but waiting can be even harder, particularly when you don't get any instant, slick answers. We've all heard the old one about the light at the end of the tunnel really being a freight train coming straight at us! But for some folks, the latest tongue-in-cheek line is:

> DUE TO THE CURRENT BUDGET CUTBACKS
> THE LIGHT AT THE END OF THE TUNNEL
> WILL BE TURNED OFF UNTIL FURTHER NOTICE.

And beyond that, things can get so dark for others they just shrug their shoulders and say, "What light? I haven't even FOUND the tunnel!"

Why You Should Always Keep a Light On

One night when Bill was not home from work yet, I looked out the window, thankful that I could see lights in the windows of neighbors' houses nearby because they made me feel less alone. If eyes are the windows of the soul, lights are the life-sparkle of a house. I even feel all warm and cozy when Tom Bodett ends his pitch for Motel 6 with "WE'LL KEEP THE LIGHT ON FOR YOU." There is something hopeful about lights in the darkness. I think we owe it to passers-by to have a light burning in the window—even if it's just a tiny one.

I remember when Larry telephoned me to say he was going to disown his family and change his name, and that he never wanted to see any of us again. The last words I spoke to him in that phone conversation—and it would be the last words I would say to him for many years—were, "The porch light will always be on for you."[1]

Somehow the symbol of keeping a light on means that we are planning to make someone WELCOME. A light in the window is like a bright star in the sky; it reminds us someone is always WAITING to welcome us home.

We all need a "light in the window" to mark the path that can illuminate our spirit. In *Sarah: Plain and Tall*, a Hallmark Hall of Fame movie made for television, Glenn Close, who played Sarah, was comforted while living on the bleak prairies of Kansas when she saw a far-away light. That flickering light showed that *someone* was out there and she wasn't totally alone.

There is an old story about a huge ship plowing through the seas in the dark of night with its signal light blinking. The captain of the ship sees another light in the distance and he blinks out an emergency message that says:

> "EMERGENCY! COLLISION INEVITABLE! CHANGE YOUR COURSE TEN DEGREES TO THE SOUTH!"

The light in the distance blinks back an answer:
> "EMERGENCY! COLLISION INEVITABLE! CHANGE YOUR COURSE TEN DEGREES TO THE NORTH!"

The captain gets a bit hot under the collar and he sends back the same message, adding,
> "I AM A CAPTAIN!"

To which the light in the distance replies:
> "EMERGENCY! COLLISION INEVITABLE! CHANGE YOUR COURSE TEN DEGREES TO THE NORTH. I AM A THIRD-CLASS SEAMAN!"

By now the captain is furious. He sends back what he believes will be the clincher to the argument:
> "EMERGENCY! EMERGENCY! COLLISION INEVITABLE! CHANGE YOUR COURSE TEN DEGREES TO THE SOUTH! I AM A BATTLESHIP!"

And the answer comes back from that blinking light in the distance:
> "EMERGENCY! COLLISION INEVITABLE! CHANGE YOUR COURSE TEN DEGREES TO THE NORTH! *I AM A LIGHTHOUSE!*"

Our Lighthouse Is Always There

Telling that story in my meetings[2] usually gets lots of chuckles, but beyond the humor you can find tremendous encouragement. We have to remember that our lighthouse, which never moves or changes, is always there for us. And the beacon that reaches out across the waves is Jesus Himself, the Light of the World.

God's light shines in the darkness, making us aware of danger. It gives us encouragement to sail on through every storm. One of my favorite psalms says, "Your Word is a lamp to my feet and a light for my path" (Ps. 119:105 NIV). I believe we pray because we are looking for light—the knowledge of how to walk through life. And yet the question persists. WHEN is Jesus going to answer our prayers? I don't know. He may answer yours tomorrow, or He may take eleven years as He did for me. Whatever happens, we have to be content:

WE KNOW GOD HAS THE ANSWERS—
HE'S JUST NOT TELLING.

But we also know that nothing enters our lives until it first passes through God's filter. While the answers may be slow in coming, *God's light is always shining.*

Letters arrive in my mailbox every day telling me that God's light is more important than getting a quick answer. One note came from a young mom who suffers terribly with chronic fatigue immune dysfunction—as she puts it, "a long name for what we don't know!" Her letter says, "The real story is God's work in me and my family's life. His grace is abundant and He gives peace that surpasses my understanding. My motto has been, 'It doesn't matter what the struggle is; what matters is how you respond.'"

And that brings us full circle to the key message of this book: keeping an upbeat attitude as we respond to what life may bring. Remember:

GOD HAS NOT PROMISED SUN WITHOUT RAIN,
JOY WITHOUT SORROW,
PEACE WITHOUT PAIN.

Do You Have Trouble with the "F Word"?

Nothing can squash a positive attitude faster than *unforgiveness*. A lot of folks struggle with this. They know they should *forgive*, but it isn't easy. For example, one gal wrote:

You asked for opinions on the *Gloomees* book. I have read and am now rereading it, as I have done all your books. I lost my mother a couple of years ago, and it has helped (is helping) me through my loss. I was her caregiver for many years.

I saw her daily, did her washing, took her out to lunch, etc. Her brothers and sisters lived a distance away so it was not convenient for them to visit. My step-siblings live a few hours' drive away—but never visited, never inquired as to her health, etc. When she died, they just dismissed the whole subject—like her life never meant anything to them.

She was such a lively person, well-educated, industrious, and loving. So, no one could (or would) help me get over the loss. I guess I've really been harboring a grudge against all of the family for their attitudes. Now, *Gloomees* has helped me begin to see the other side of the coin. I have underlined the sentence "To carry a load of guilt [or in my case—resentment] around with you after a loved one is gone is wasted energy."

Another letter comes from a young woman who had lost every important man in her life. Her father had died in Vietnam; two brothers died in a plane crash. By the time she was thirty she had three children and was going through a divorce from an adulterous husband. ("OUCH! That was the LAST STRAW!" she wrote.) She was ready to give up on life, but rededication to the Lord and having three small children to care for kept her going. Her letter continued:

Romans 8:28 got me through that divorce. I clung to that verse like a child clings to a teddy bear. It was truly amazing what one little verse did for my breaking heart. And the statement you made that God never fails: *Nothing happens by chance in life,* but is planned by God—I know the truth in that little piece of wisdom.

I am now married to a wonderful Christian husband who adores the ground I walk on. In his previous marriage he went through the same thing I did. God brought us together and has created a bond of love that cannot be broken.

I guess my life sounds pretty rosy today. Mostly it is, but I have really been struggling with the "F word"—*forgiveness*. I get so angry with what my first husband did to me. I have talked with people at church about it, and I have prayed about it. I thought I'd really forgiven him, yet I continue to have spiteful, unloving feelings toward him.

Your books are really opening my eyes in a way no one else has done. I'm realizing that to fully enjoy today's blessings, I have to put the past behind me. . . I have learned in my life that trials are wonderful gifts from the Lord. They mold us, strengthen us, and we grow into the individual the Lord wants us to become. Some of us are just destined to be survivors and I accept that. . . . Thanks for the encouragement, the love, the conviction, and, most importantly, the laughter.

One of my favorite letters came from a mom who told me *Geranium* encouraged her to change her attitude. She said, "I do not want to get a case of 'hardening of the attitudes' through unforgiveness, bitterness, or for any other causes. . . . I will purpose in my heart to try to find more humor, give more of myself to others, and give everything to God in prayer. I have been abundantly blessed, and I KNOW God has a future of hope, not of calamity, planned for each of us."

Yes, it's true that we may ask for answers, but God doesn't always supply them. But it is HOW we respond to our problems that counts, not having perfect solutions. That's why Jesus told us to keep asking, seeking, and knocking: "For everyone who asks receives; he who seeks finds; and to him who knocks, the door will be opened." [3] And all the while we ask, seek, and knock, we remember that *all things*—the pain, problems, frustrations, and even the doldrums of life—work together for good for those who love God and who want to be part of His plans.

We may go without specific answers indefinitely, but we can still rejoice. We can have hope, and we can even laugh because we know that His LIGHT is always enough!

The following letter, from a twenty-two-year-old girl, is one of the most encouraging I have ever received. She mentioned reading *Gloomees* and learning of the number of letters I get

lord ... make me quick to forgive and quicker still to ask forgiveness ...

forgive my hidden faults ... Psa 19:12

© "Sonshine Promises" created by Gretchen Clasby, Cedar Hill Studio.
Used by permission.

from parents sharing the sharp disappointment they feel because of a wayward child. Then she went on to say:

> I want to encourage those parents to PRAY, PRAY, PRAY,
> AND PRAY SOME MORE!!!! I was one of those wayward
> children, but I've made my way to the Lord. Both my parents are mighty prayer warriors! I know without a doubt
> that it was their prayers that brought me to my knees
> ready to repent!!!
>
> I was an alcoholic, a smoker, had started to do drugs, and
> was sexually active throughout high school. I thought I
> knew everything. I got involved with the "wrong" kind of
> friends and was very mean and manipulative. One day as
> my father stood picketing an abortion clinic, I marched into
> the clinic with my nose in the air and killed his grandchild.
>
> Did they forgive me? With God's grace, yes, they did!!
> Through Christian counseling and many tears we've restored our relationship. I've been sober and clean for two
> years now, I teach Sunday school and share my testimony
> whenever I can. I enjoy being with my parents; when we're

together we laugh a ton. I'm now married to an incredible, godly, forgiving man who knows all about my past and still loves me anyway.

I know there were days when my parents felt their prayers were not being heard, let alone not being answered, but they kept praying and trusting Christ. In *HIS* perfect timing, I made my commitment to Christ and the uphill climb to restoration and healing. There will be days when the dark tunnel will go on and on for miles, but just re-member—there is light at the end of it, God's light!

I hope this young gal's words encourage you as much as they did me. She is a product of God's grace, which is always at work no matter how dark things get. Fear keeps us limping in the dark, but grace keeps us walking in the light. Remember this:

GOD HAS NOT PROMISED TO GIVE US ALL
THE ANSWERS,
BUT HE HAS PROMISED HIS GRACE.

Not long ago I heard a sermon on Jesus' familiar promise, "Abide in Me, and I in you."[4] I realized that the Lord's words enable me to say in every circumstance, *"For THIS I need Jesus."* And then I always hear His answer: *"Don't worry—for THIS you have Me."*

You see, He is with us in the darkness just as surely as He is in the light. When we trust HIM, the dark clouds of trouble are but the shadow of HIS WINGS, and we can pray:

LORD,
I JUST DON'T UNDERSTAND
WHAT IN THE WORLD
YOU'RE DOING IN MY LIFE,

and back will come His answer:

MY CHILD,
DON'T TRY TO UNDERSTAND.
JUST LIVE IT
FOR ME.

Ruth Harms Calkin[5]

"Suzy's Zoo" illustration © '86 Suzy Spafford. Used by permission.

Endnotes

Introduction   Mama, Get the What?
1. "Mama, Get the Hammer, There's a Fly on Papa's Head" by Frank Davis and Walter Bishop. Copyright © 1961 by Southern Music Publishing Co., Inc. Copyright renewed. All rights reserved. Used by permission. International copyright renewed.

2. This woman's letter was originally mentioned in Barbara Johnson, *Stick a Geranium in Your Hat and Be Happy* (Dallas: Word, 1990), 56.

3. Dave Barry with Roger Yepsen, ed., *Babies and Other Hazards of Sex* (Emmaus, Pa.: Rodale, 1984).

Chapter 1   The Head Thinks, the Hands Labor, But It's the Heart That Laughs
1. The book is *Stick a Geranium in Your Hat and Be Happy*. We often refer to it as simply *Geranium*.

2. Printed in the monthly newsletter published by Westcoast Printing, 2383 S. Tamiami Trail, Venice, Florida 34293.

3. See the *Mayo Clinic Health Letter*, March 1993, which recaps an article on laughter appearing in *The Journal of the American Medical Association*, 1 April 1992.

4. Annette Goodheart, Ph.D., "Laughter Your Way to Health," video produced by Goodheart, Inc., P. O. Box 40297, Santa Barbara, California 93140.

5. Victor Borge, quoted in *Mayo Clinic Health Letter*, March 1993.

6. See James 1:12 NIV.

7. Adapted from an article in the *Toronto Sun*, 26 July 1977.

8. Roger Shouse, pastor of Greenwood Church of Christ, Greenwood, Indiana. Used by permission.

9. Gertrude Mayhew, *Reminisce*, November/December 1992, 59.

10. These two bumper snickers are included here courtesy of Stan Grams, editor of *The Mountain Ear*, the bulletin of the Rotary Club of Gatlinburg, Tennessee.

11. Thanks to Roger Shouse, pastor of Greenwood Church of Christ, Greenwood, Indiana.

12. From the Remarkable Things catalog, Long Beach, California. Used by permission.

13. Thanks to freelance writer Sherrie Weaver of Denver, Colorado, for permission to use her Updated Witticisms.

14. Avis P. Agin, "A Few Lighthearted Sayings That Have the Ring of Truth," *Arizona Senior World*, date unknown.

15. Ibid.

16. Adapted from a column by Dr. Peter Gott, syndicated by Newspaper Enterprise Association. Used by permission of Dr. Gott.

17. *The Living Bible* translation of Proverbs 15:15 is paraphrased slightly in the feminine gender.

Chapter 2   Some Days You're the Pigeon, Some Days You're the Statue

1. 2 Cor. 4:8–9 NIV.

2. Catherine Feste, *The Physician Within: Taking Charge of Your Well-Being*, (Minneapolis: Diabetes Center, Inc., 1987), 88.

3. See Eph. 6:11–18.

4. This story was used in a sermon by Dr. William R. McElwee of the Haddonfield, New Jersey, United Methodist Church. Used here by permission.

5. Pat Hanson, ed., "Pat Prints," (Chippewa Falls, Wisc.) 1993.

6. Thanks to freelance writer Sherri Weaver of Denver, Colorado, for permission to use her Updated Witticism.

7. Isa. 49:16 NIV, paraphrased.

Chapter 3   I Know a Little Suffering Is Good for the Soul, But Somebody Must Be Trying to Make a Saint Out of Me!

1. See, for example, 2 Sam. 12:15–23 and 18:32–33.
2. John 11:17–35.
3. Luke 19:41–44.
4. William Shakespeare, *The Third Part of King Henry VI*.
5. Alfred, Lord Tennyson, *The Princess*, Song VI, "Home They Brought Her Warrior," stanza 1.
6. See Barbara Johnson, *Stick a Geranium In Your Hat and Be Happy*, chapter 3, and Barbara Johnson, *Splashes of Joy in the Cesspools of Life* (Dallas: Word Publishing, 1992), chapter 3.
7. For accounts of my near suicide, see *Stick a Geranium in Your Hat and Be Happy*, 47–48, and *Splashes of Joy in the Cesspools of Life*, 57–59.
8. Because support groups are so important, they are discussed in more detail in chapter 5.
9. In *Splashes of Joy in the Cesspools of Life* I described how I ride my stationary bicycle in my Joy Room, a part of my mobile home that's packed with mementos and gag gifts. As I ride I have a big map of the United States in front of me, and I make imaginary trips to Spatula friends who have written to me.
10. This is a paraphrase of a line from Audrey Meier's song, "He Washed My Eyes with Tears," published by Manna Music.

Chapter 4   Yesterday Is Experience . . . Tomorrow Is Hope . . . Today Is Getting from One to the Other

1. Ruth Harms Calkin, *Lord, You Love to Say Yes* (Elgin, Ill.: David C. Cook Publishing Co., 1976), 105. Used by permission.
2. Prov. 11:25, paraphrased.
3. This idea is credited to the Roman playwright Terence (Publius Terentius Afer).
4. "Hope Is the Thing with Feathers," in *The Complete Poems of Emily Dickinson* (New York: Little, Brown and Co., n.d.), 116. Used by permission.

Chapter 5   Cast Your Bread Upon the Waters and It Will Come Back Pretzels
1. Eccles. 4:10 NIV.
2. See Luke 15:17 NIV.
3. Dick Innes, *Servant* (a ministry of Prairie Bible Institute), Nov./Dec. 1993, 11. Used by permission.
4. Eccles. 4:12 NIV.
5. Helen Steiner Rice, "The Gift of Friendship," *Gifts from the Heart* (Old Tappan: Fleming H. Revell, 1981), 38. Used by permission.
6. Agin, *Arizona Senior World.*

Chapter 6   If the Sky Falls Tomorrow, Have Clouds for Breakfast
1. Num. 32:23 NIV.
2. See Rom. 12:3 and Phil. 2:3 NIV.
3. Patsy Clairmont, *Normal Is the Setting On a Dryer* (Colorado Springs: Focus on the Family, 1993).
4. Contributed by Evelyn Heinz. Used by permission.

Chapter 7   Life Is a Great Big Canvas . . . Throw All the Paint on It You Can
1. For more ideas for celebrating life, see Alexandra Stoddard, *Living a Beautiful Life* (New York: Random House, 1986).

Chapter 8   Year-Long Resolutions: Hope for the Best, Be Prepared for the Worst, Take What Comes with a Smile
1. Adapted from the Serenity Prayer by Reinhold Niebuhr.
2. Joel Goodman, quoted in the *Hudson Valley (N.Y.) Sunday Record,* 27 March 1988, 102.
3. Dr. James Read, "Health Care Providers Turn to Humor," *The Free China Journal,* 23 February 1989.
4. Louisa Fletcher, "The Land of Beginning Again," *Best-Loved Poems* (Garden City, N.Y.: Doubleday, 1936).
5. Prov. 11:25, paraphrased.

6. Norma Wiltse, Allegheny, New York. Used by permission.

7. Adapted from Adair Lara, "Conspiracy of Kindness," *Glamour*, December 1991, 86.

8. Franklin P. Jones, quoted in Dr. Laurence J. Peter, *Peter's Quotations* (New York: William Morrow & Co., 1977), 102.

9. Edward Whiting, *Sunshine Magazine*, n.d.

Conclusion   Life Ain't No Ride on No Pink Duck, But So What!

1. See Johnson, *Stick a Geranium in Your Hat and Be Happy*, 52.

2. I also shared the lighthouse story in *Fresh Elastic for Stretched-Out Moms* (Grand Rapids: Revell, 1986), 52.

3. See Matt. 7:7–8 NIV.

4. John 15:4 NKJV.

5. Ruth Harms Calkin, *Lord, It Keeps Happening and Happening* (Wheaton: Tyndale House, Living Books, 1984), 100. Used by permission.